Cambridge Elements

Elements in the Archaeology of Ancient Israel
edited by
Aaron A. Burke
University of California, Los Angeles
Jeremy D. Smoak
University of California, Los Angeles

BETWEEN YAHWISM AND JUDAISM

Judean Cult and Culture during the Early Hellenistic Period (332–175 BCE)

Yonatan Adler
Ariel University

Shaftesbury Road, Cambridge CB2 8EA, United Kingdom

One Liberty Plaza, 20th Floor, New York, NY 10006, USA

477 Williamstown Road, Port Melbourne, VIC 3207, Australia

314–321, 3rd Floor, Plot 3, Splendor Forum, Jasola District Centre, New Delhi – 110025, India

103 Penang Road, #05–06/07, Visioncrest Commercial, Singapore 238467

Cambridge University Press is part of Cambridge University Press & Assessment, a department of the University of Cambridge.

We share the University's mission to contribute to society through the pursuit of education, learning and research at the highest international levels of excellence.

www.cambridge.org
Information on this title: www.cambridge.org/9781009459624

DOI: 10.1017/9781009459594

© Yonatan Adler 2025

This publication is in copyright. Subject to statutory exception and to the provisions of relevant collective licensing agreements, no reproduction of any part may take place without the written permission of Cambridge University Press & Assessment.

When citing this work, please include a reference to the DOI 10.1017/9781009459594

First published 2025

A catalogue record for this publication is available from the British Library

ISBN 978-1-009-45962-4 Hardback
ISBN 978-1-009-45961-7 Paperback
ISSN 2754-3013 (online)
ISSN 2754-3005 (print)

Cambridge University Press & Assessment has no responsibility for the persistence or accuracy of URLs for external or third-party internet websites referred to in this publication and does not guarantee that any content on such websites is, or will remain, accurate or appropriate.

For EU product safety concerns, contact us at Calle de José Abascal, 56, 1°, 28003 Madrid, Spain, or email eugpsr@cambridge.org

Between Yahwism and Judaism

Judean Cult and Culture during the Early Hellenistic Period (332–175 BCE)

Elements in the Archaeology of Ancient Israel

DOI: 10.1017/9781009459594
First published online: September 2025

Yonatan Adler
Ariel University
Author for correspondence: Yonatan Adler, yonatanadler@gmail.com

> **Abstract:** This Element seeks to characterize key aspects of the cult and culture of the Judean populace at large, in Judea and the diaspora, during the Early Hellenistic period (332–175 BCE). It asks if this period signals cultural *continuity* with the Yahwism of the past, or cultural *rupture* with the emergence of Judaism as known from later times. It investigates administrative structures, whether Torah was widely observed, how and where Judeans performed cultic worship of YHWH and if this had become exclusive of other deities, adoption of Greek cultural elements and what literature was well-known and influential, including "biblical" literature. It concludes that while no rupture is evident, and the Early Hellenistic period marks a strong degree of continuity with the Yahwism of Persian times, in some senses the era paved a way for the subsequent transition into the Judaism of the future.

Keywords: Judaism, Yahwism, Early Hellenistic period, cult, culture

© Yonatan Adler 2025

ISBNs: 9781009459624 (HB), 9781009459617 (PB), 9781009459594 (OC)
ISSNs: 2754-3013 (online), 2754-3005 (print)

Contents

1 Introduction 1

2 Administrative Structures 14

3 Torah Law 25

4 Cultic Worship of YHWH 35

5 Adoption of Greek Cultural Elements 48

6 Literary Reception 59

7 Conclusions 65

List of Abbreviations 69

References 70

1 Introduction

This Element aims to characterize key aspects of the cult and culture of the Judeans, both in their ancestral homeland and throughout their diaspora communities, during the Early Hellenistic period (332–175 BCE). Its chronological scope opens with the Macedonian conquest of the Levant from the Persian Empire in 332 BCE and closes with the death of Seleucus IV Philopator in 175 BCE and the subsequent ascension of his brother, Antiochus IV Epiphanes, to the throne of the Seleucid Empire. This is a sociocultural study, focused on cultural shifts within Judean society at large rather than on literary or intellectual trends. The central question to be explored here is to what degree Judean cult and culture during this historical period reflect *continuity* with Yahwism of the past and to what extent they signal an era of *rupture* with the emergence of something like a nascent Judaism.

This introductory section presents background information and further details about the aims and scope of the present volume. It opens with a brief survey of the historical timeline and geopolitical background to the Early Hellenistic period (Figure 1). It then introduces what is meant when one speaks of "Judeans" as an identity group at this time, and provides some background to the Judean communities spread throughout the Early Hellenistic world. This is followed by a survey of the state of the question within scholarship surrounding the nature of Judean cult and culture during this period, and regarding the utility of the terms "Yahwism" and "Judaism." Next, the section outlines the primary sources of surviving data which shed light on the contours of Judean cult and culture at this time and which will be interrogated here: archaeological, numismatic, papyrological, epigraphic, and literary. It closes with an outline of the structure and contents of the present study.

1.1 Historical Timeline and Geopolitical Background

Alexander the Great of Macedonia (reigned 336–323 BCE) launched his invasion of the Persian Empire in 334 BCE, crossing the Hellespont and commencing a series of successful military campaigns throughout the Achaemenid realm and beyond.[1] His armies conquered the Levant and Egypt in 332 BCE, and the following year marched eastward to take Mesopotamia and Persia. In the ensuing years, Alexander's troops moved into territories in Central Asia and the Indian subcontinent. At the time of his death in 323 BCE, his armies controlled a vast territory stretching from Greece and the Balkans in the northwest, to the Indus Valley in the east, and over to Egypt in the southwest.

---

[1] As the details of the cursory historical overview provided here are well-known, it will suffice to cite the convenient historical synthesis provided in Shipley (2000).

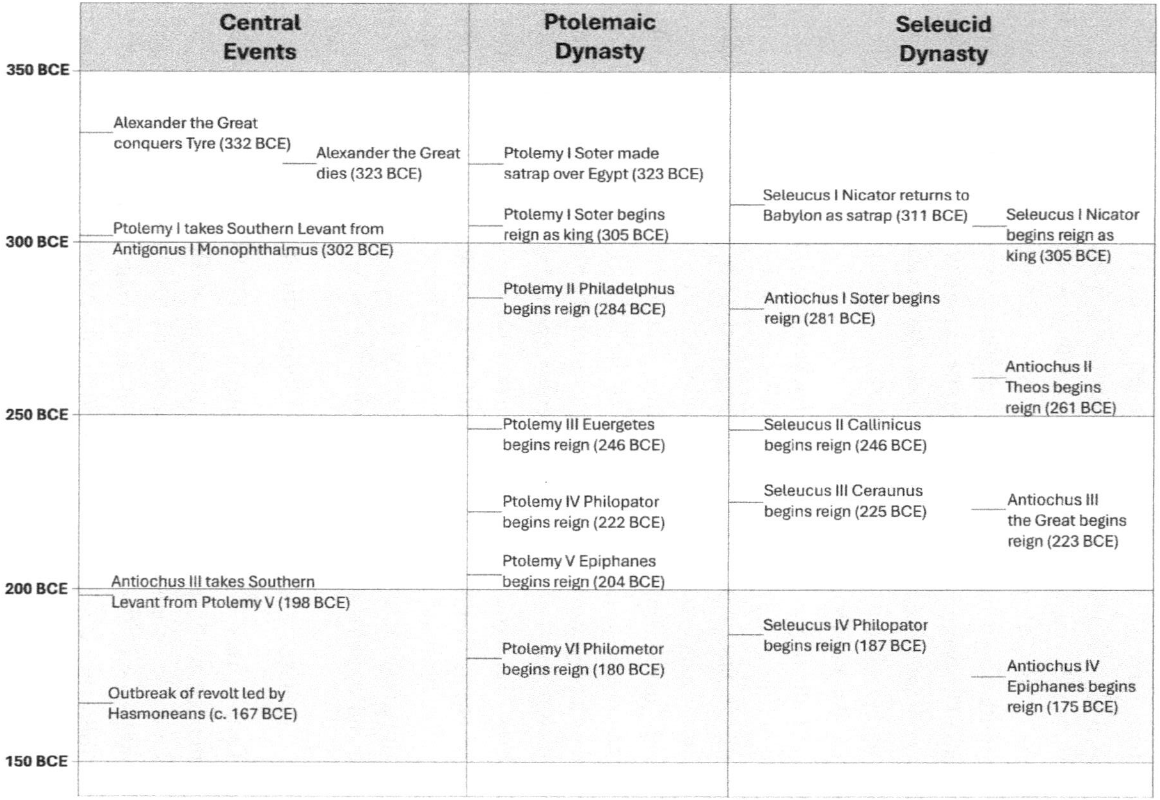

	Central Events	Ptolemaic Dynasty	Seleucid Dynasty
350 BCE	Alexander the Great conquers Tyre (332 BCE) — Alexander the Great dies (323 BCE)	Ptolemy I Soter made satrap over Egypt (323 BCE)	
300 BCE	Ptolemy I takes Southern Levant from Antigonus I Monophthalmus (302 BCE)	Ptolemy I Soter begins reign as king (305 BCE) — Ptolemy II Philadelphus begins reign (284 BCE)	Seleucus I Nicator returns to Babylon as satrap (311 BCE) — Seleucus I Nicator begins reign as king (305 BCE) — Antiochus I Soter begins reign (281 BCE)
250 BCE		Ptolemy III Euergetes begins reign (246 BCE) — Ptolemy IV Philopator begins reign (222 BCE) — Ptolemy V Epiphanes begins reign (204 BCE)	Antiochus II Theos begins reign (261 BCE) — Seleucus II Callinicus begins reign (246 BCE) — Seleucus III Ceraunus begins reign (225 BCE) — Antiochus III the Great begins reign (223 BCE)
200 BCE	Antiochus III takes Southern Levant from Ptolemy V (198 BCE) — Outbreak of revolt led by Hasmoneans (c. 167 BCE)	Ptolemy VI Philometor begins reign (180 BCE)	Seleucus IV Philopator begins reign (187 BCE) — Antiochus IV Epiphanes begins reign (175 BCE)
150 BCE			

Figure 1 Timeline of the Hellenistic period (after Shipley 2000: xxv–xxix).

As Alexander left no clear heir, his empire descended into decades of internal struggles between his generals, known as the Diadochi (Greek: *Diádokhoi*, meaning "Successors"). The initial conflicts, lasting from 322 to 301 BCE, led to the establishment of the major Hellenistic kingdoms. Although initially ruling as "satraps" over the different regions of the divided empire, eventually each of the Diadochi came to reign as "king" over the territory under his control. Ptolemy I Soter (reigned 305/304–283 BCE) founded a kingdom in Egypt, and ruled out of Alexandria. Initially, Antigonus I Monophthalmus (reigned 306–301 BCE) came to control much of Western Asia, but by 311 BCE, he had lost Mesopotamia, Persia, and the eastern territories in Central Asia to Seleucus I Nicator (reigned 305/304–281 BCE). The Southern Levant sat at a crossroads between territories and changed hands several times between Ptolemy and Antigonus, with the latter holding onto the territory continuously from 312 to 302 BCE. In 302 BCE, Ptolemy wrested the Southern Levant and Phoenicia from Antigonus, and in the following year, Antigonus was ruinously attacked by Seleucus, joined by two of the other Diadochi: Cassander (reigned 305/304–297 BCE) out of Macedonia and Greece and Lysimachus (reigned 305/304–281 BCE) out of Thrace. The three allies defeated and killed Antigonus in the pivotal Battle of Ipsus in 301 BCE, after which his remaining territories were divided between Seleucus, who took Syria and eastern Anatolia, and Lysimachus, who took western Anatolia.

The following century saw Ptolemy and his descendants establish an enduring dynasty in Egypt, and Seleucus and his descendants a stable royal line in Western Asia. The Ptolemies' capital city remained in Alexandria throughout, while the Seleucids ruled first out of Seleucia-on-the-Tigris (just south of modern Baghdad) and later out of Antioch-on-the-Orontes (modern Antakya in Turkey). The two kingdoms became embroiled in a series of six wars, known as the Syrian Wars, primarily over control of the region encompassing the Southern Levant and Phoenicia. The first four wars ended with the Ptolemaic kingdom retaining control over this region, but the Fifth Syrian War (201–198 BCE) ended with the Seleucid king Antiochus III Megas (reigned 223–187 BCE) conquering the contested territory.

The early second century BCE saw Antiochus and his heir, Seleucus IV Philopator (reigned 187–175 BCE), maintain uncontested sovereignty over the Southern Levant and Phoenicia, which came to be known as Coele-Syria (Greek: *Koílē Suría*, meaning "the hollow of Syria"). The assassination of Seleucus in 175 BCE marked the end of an era of relative stability for the Seleucid dynasty, and the start of a slow but steady demise of the kingdom. Heliodorus, a powerful Seleucid official who may have been behind the assassination, briefly took over as regent on behalf of Seleucus' young child Antiochus. Heliodorus' reign as regent was brief, however; months later, he was replaced by Antiochus IV Epiphanes (reigned 175–164 BCE), brother of Seleucus. Antiochus' rule was marred by a humiliating setback in 168 BCE during the sixth and final of the Syrian Wars, when a single Roman ambassador forced the Seleucid king to retreat from what had been a successful march on Alexandria. The following years witnessed the eruption of a revolt in Judea, led by brothers belonging to the priestly Hasmonean clan. The decades following the death of Antiochus in 164 BCE saw a series of warring contenders to the throne further weaken the grip of the Seleucid monarchy over the vast territories under its control, including Judea, which achieved full autonomy in 142 BCE under the last survivor among the Hasmonean brothers, Simon Thassi (ruled 142–134 BCE).

1.2 "Judean" Identity in the Early Hellenistic World

In texts dating to the first half of the first millennium BCE, we begin to encounter a group that both self-identified and was referred to by others using a name formed from the consonantal root "*y-h-d*." Among the earliest appearances of the name are references to King Hezekiah "the Judean" (*Ia-ú-da-a-a*) in Akkadian texts from around the end of the eighth century BCE (Chicago Prism II:76; Taylor Prism II:71–72; Bull 4:23, 27; Letter to the God Ashur 4; English transliterations and translations collected in Mayer 2003). Later texts in the Hebrew Bible refer to this group in Hebrew as "*yəhûdîm*" (e.g., 2 Kgs 16:6; Jer 32:12; 34:9), and Aramaic texts from the latter half of the fifth century BCE at Elephantine (in southern Egypt) render the name as "*yəhûdāyē*'" (e.g., *TAD*, A4.1:1, 10; A4.7:19, 22, 26). The name is rendered into Greek as "*Ioudaîoi*" in the writings of Greek authors beginning in the late fourth and early third centuries BCE (e.g., Theophr., *Piet.*, apud: Porph., *Abst.* 2.26; Megasthenes, *Indica*, apud: Clem. Al., *Strom.* 15:72:5) and in documentary papyri from Egypt from the middle of the third century BCE (e.g., *CPJ* 1, no. 8:5; 9:2). We will henceforth use the English term "Judeans" when referring to those who would have identified in ancient languages as *yəhûdîm/yəhûdāyē'/Ioudaîoi*.[2]

It seems almost certain that, in the beginning, the term "Judeans" applied exclusively to people living within the land of Judea. However, following the

---

[2] In recent years, a rather curious debate has developed within English language scholarship about which name is most suitable when referring to this group in the ancient past (e.g., Cohen 1999: 3, 69–70, 104–5; Mason 2007; Schwartz 2007; Schwartz 2011). There seems to be a common assumption among those engaged in this dispute that the modern English word "Jew" signifies some religious character, as it is commonly located within the same semantic category as "Christian" and "Muslim." As such, so the argument goes, it is appropriate to use the term "Jews" only when considering a time after this group had developed a specifically religious identity, while prior to this time it is preferable to refer to these people as "Judeans." The key question that divides these scholars is exactly when in historical time this supposed seminal

Assyrian and Babylonian incursions into Judea (ca. 701 and 586 BCE, respectively) and the destruction and exiles which ensued, we begin to find communities of people identifying as Judeans in regions far removed from the Judean homeland. In Babylonia, we have ample primary evidence for Judean communities from early in the sixth century until the very end of the fifth century BCE (Alstola 2020). While direct, primary evidence of Judeans in Mesopotamia from the Hellenistic period is largely lacking, it seems likely that Judean communities continued to thrive in Mesopotamia throughout this time (Hegermann 1989: 145–46). In Egypt, we have abundant evidence for thriving communities of people identifying as Judeans beginning in the Persian era, evidence which increases significantly into the Hellenistic and Roman periods (Kasher 1985). Elsewhere in the eastern Mediterranean, Judean communities were thriving in Syria, Anatolia, the Balkans, the Greek mainland, and the isles of the Aegean by the first century BCE and the first century CE. While direct evidence for the presence of Judeans in these regions in earlier periods is sparse, the limited evidence that *has* survived suggests that many of these later Judean communities may trace their beginnings to the Early Hellenistic period (if not to the Persian period) (Hegermann 1989: 146–51). If this was indeed the case, then groups of Judeans would have been found not only – or even primarily – in the Judean homeland, but also throughout much of both the Ptolemaic and Seleucid kingdoms, as well as in other Greek-speaking territories throughout the greater region.

To be clear, the term "Judean," as it will be used here, refers to an identity group formed of individuals who saw themselves as in some way connected to one another, and as in some way associated with the land of Judea – whether as their current place of residence or through some form of historic ties (true or imagined). The term makes no a priori assumptions about any specific beliefs, cultic practices, or cultural features; it is precisely these matters that are to be explored in this Element.

1.3 The State of the Question

Much of scholarship which has explored cultic and cultural aspects of Judean society during the Early Hellenistic period has operated under a paradigm that presumed the laws of the Torah were already widely known and observed by this time as a societal norm among Judeans both in their homeland and throughout their diaspora communities. Working under this presumption,

---

movement from "Judeans" to "Jews" might have taken place. In this Element, I will use the term "Judeans" when referring to members of the identity group known in ancient languages as *yəhûdîm*/*yəhûdāyē'*/*Ioudaioi* – with no intention toward any supposed "religious" implication this term may or may not hold.

scholars have supposed that various Early Hellenistic kings allowed Judeans to be autonomously organized and adjudicated according to Torah legislation (Tcherikover 1957: 7, 1959: 305–6; Mélèze-Modrzejewski 1996, 2001; Bickerman 2007a: 355). Also under this model, it has been widely assumed that at this time Judeans were venerating YHWH to the exclusion of all other deities (e.g., Tcherikover 1959: 83–4, 305; Grabbe 2008a: 255–56), and that the cult of YHWH was centralized at the Jerusalem temple to the exclusion of any other cultic site (see Runesson 2001: 403–28, where this common presupposition is critiqued). The assumption of widespread Torah observance at this time is also taken as the starting point for exploring the encounter between "Judaism," thus envisioned, and contemporary Greek culture (e.g., Hengel 1974). And the idea that by this time the Pentateuch, along with other biblical texts, already enjoyed widespread reception among Judeans, both in their homeland and in the diaspora, led to the hypothesis that the project of translating these writings into Greek was motivated by the need of Greek-speaking Judean communities for accessible educational and liturgical texts (e.g., Dorival 1988: 67–71).

The roots of this paradigm may be traced back to nineteenth-century biblical scholarship, which posited that the Babylonian exile marked a distinct watershed in the religion and culture of the Judeans. The books of Ezra-Nehemiah tell of the Persian king Artaxerxes sending Ezra, a Judean scribe, on a mission from Babylon to Jerusalem to promulgate and enforce the divine law of the Judeans upon the inhabitants of Judea (Ezra 7:1–28). Ezra is said to have completed this royal assignment by reading from "the book of the instruction of Moses [sēfer tôrat mōšeh], which YHWH had commanded Israel" before a mass gathering of Judeans in Jerusalem (Neh 8:1–18). Taking these narratives at face value, W. M. L. de Wette (1813: 1:148) regarded the Persian era as a turning point: "We must view the nation after the exile as a different one, with a different worldview and religion." He argued that the preexilic people should be called "Hebrews" (Hebräer) and their culture "Hebraism" (Hebraismus), while the postexilic people should be called "Jews" (Juden) and their culture "Judaism" (Judenthum). De Wette's model of a radical rupture during the Achaemenid period proved extremely influential upon subsequent biblical scholarship. This is especially evident in the work of Julius Wellhausen, who established as the aim of his Prolegomena to show that the promulgation of the Pentateuch as Torah law in the Persian period marks the endpoint of "ancient Israel" (altes Israel) (equivalent to de Wette's "Hebraism") and the starting point of "Judaism" (Judentum) (Wellhausen 1885: 1–13). This model had ramifications not only for biblical scholars and historians working on the Persian period but also for scholars whose work focused on the subsequent Hellenistic period. If the Torah had become the authoritative law of the Judeans by the fifth century BCE, so the thinking went, certainly it must have remained so throughout the subsequent centuries.

Recent years have seen a growing reluctance among specialists of the Achaemenid period to rely on the biblical narratives about Ezra's supposed promulgation of the Torah as a valid lens for interpreting primary data from this time. Scholars examining the Persian-era archaeological record from Judea, for example, have begun to question whether the data truly suggest a "religious revolution" at this time, as had been posited in the past (Frevel, Pyschny, and Cornelius 2014). Others looking at the epigraphic and papyrological record from Elephantine and the epigraphic record from Mesopotamia have opted to analyze this data on its own terms rather than through the lens of the Hebrew Bible (Kratz 2015, 2020; Granerød 2016, 2019; Barnea 2021; Adler 2022). Rather than speaking about "Judaism" in the Persian period (which usually implies widespread adherence to Torah law), scholars have increasingly begun to prefer the term "Yahwism" when discussing the cult and culture of Judeans (and other worshipers of YHWH) during the Achaemenid period (most recently: Barnea and Kratz 2024).

Taking its cue from this recent trend in scholarship on the Achaemenid era, this Element addresses the problem of Yahwism's development into the *subsequent* era of history, following the close of the Persian period. The central question we shall explore here is to what degree did the cult and culture of Judean society in the Early Hellenistic period resemble Judean Yahwism of the Persian period, and to what degree did it begin to correspond to Judaism as it was known in the following Late Hellenistic and Roman periods. In other words: should the Early Hellenistic period be regarded as an era of cultural *continuity* with the Yahwism of the past, or should it be viewed as one of cultural *rupture* signaling the emergence of nascent Judaism as it later came to be known?

To be clear, our focus here is on Judean society at large, represented primarily by the masses of common people who composed the vast majority of the population. Accordingly, this Element will not explore the development of cultic or cultural concepts which began to emerge in the writings of Judean *literati* at this time if these cannot be shown to have been widely known and embraced by the masses of *ordinary* Judeans. In other words, the focus of this study is on *sociocultural* history rather than *intellectual* history.

1.4 Primary Sources of Data

The choice of primary sources of data to be interrogated here is circumscribed by the Element's focus on the commoners of Judean society rather than on its intellectuals. Special attention will be paid to material remains that are randomly sampled and widely distributed, as these may be regarded as representative of widespread sociocultural phenomena. This includes archaeological remains, numismatic finds, documents written on papyrus, and inscriptions on nonperishable materials such as stone and pottery. Ancient texts that have been preserved within various literary genres and passed down through time will also be investigated. Each of these data sources – both the material and the textual – comes with its own suite of methodological problems, some unique to the period and subject of our inquiry. In what follows, I will outline the various primary sources of data available to be investigated in this study, and briefly discuss some of the main methodological challenges we encounter in their analysis.

1.4.1 Archaeology

Archaeology provides one of the most reliable and potent tools for discerning actual human behaviors in the past. There are, however, several severe limitations on the quantity and quality of the archaeological data available which might be sought to shed light on Judean cult and culture in the Early Hellenistic period.

Outside of Judea, it is practically impossible to identify archaeological material from the Early Hellenistic period as having been associated with Judeans – unless this material bears an inscription attesting to such a relation. Scholarship has yet to identify any *uniquely Judean* types of pottery, small finds, architecture, or iconography from this period of time. Outside of Judea proper, there are almost no Early Hellenistic levels at archaeological sites that have been compellingly identified as having been settled or otherwise used specifically by Judeans.

This leaves the immediate province of Judea as the only region where we can expect the uninscribed material remains to manifest specifically Judean cultural traits. But here as well, we encounter significant hurdles in identifying archaeological remains as having been associated with Judeans living in the Early Hellenistic period. The two primary challenges involve defining the geographical borders of Judea and overcoming critical stratigraphic problems that hinder our ability to date archaeological levels precisely to the Early Hellenistic period.

Precious little information about the boundaries of the province of Judea during the Early Hellenistic period is available from contemporary historical sources or material remains. Instead, scholars extrapolate about the borders of the province at the end of the Early Hellenistic period from clues found in 1 Maccabees, which identify locations along what seems to have served as a military frontier of sorts between the Maccabean rebels and the Seleucid forces sent to quell the rebellion (Lipschits 2005: 146–49; Finkelstein 2018: 60–65). While this approach allows us to sketch a compelling map of the

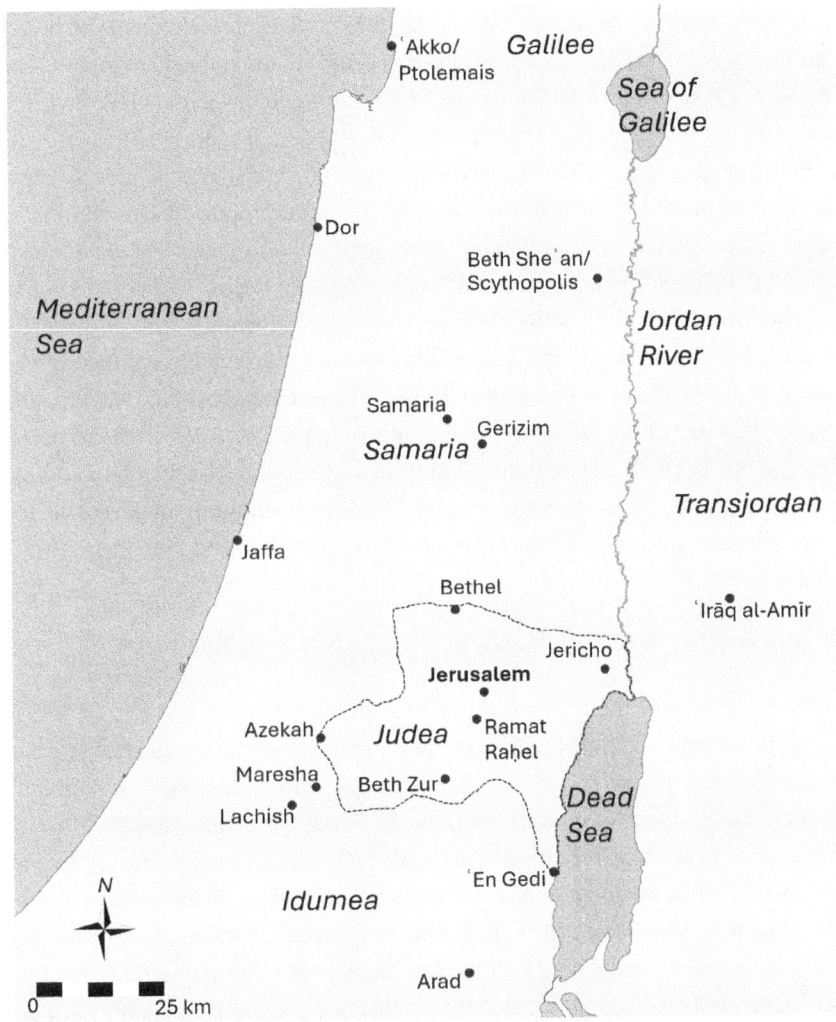

Figure 2 Map of the borders of Judea at the end of the Early Hellenistic period (after Shalom et al. 2021: 64, figure 5.1).

borders of the province around the end of the Early Hellenistic period (Figure 2), the boundaries of Judea at the beginning of the period are harder to establish and remain a matter of debate. Although some scholars believe that the borders remained essentially unchanged from the end of the Persian period until the end of the Early Hellenistic period (Lipschits 2005: 146–49), others believe that the province at the start of the Early Hellenistic period was much smaller in area, and that settlement in Judea expanded after the end of the Persian period and before the rise of the Hasmonean state (Finkelstein 2018: 60–65).

A more serious challenge is posed by the stratigraphic character of layers dating to the Persian and Early Hellenistic periods in the immediate region. The Southern Levant in general, and Judea in particular, lack significant destruction layers dating to the entire period between the early sixth century and the middle of the second century BCE (Shalom et al. 2021: 63). Without such destruction layers, it is incredibly difficult to define and date stratigraphic phases within and across sites. This has resulted in an unfortunate situation where archaeologists have usually been forced to relate to the entire period following the Babylonian destruction of 586 BCE until the rise of the Hasmoneans in the mid second century BCE in an imprecise, generalized manner. Fortunately, excavations in recent years at sites such as Ramat Raḥel, Tel Azekah, Khirbet Qeiyafa, and Ramat Bet Shemesh, along with the recent publication of excavations at Lachish and Khirbet er-Rasm, have allowed archaeologists to begin to address this stratigraphic challenge and to assign higher-resolution subphases to the long "Persian/Early Hellenistic period" (Kreimerman and Sandhaus 2021; Shalom et al. 2021).

1.4.2 Numismatics

From the middle of the fourth century BCE until perhaps as late as 242 or 241 BCE, the province of Judea minted its own silver coins with unique Hebrew and Aramaic inscriptions in paleo-Hebrew script, and with oftentimes unique graphic images and designs (Gitler, Lorber, and Fontanille 2023). Most of these coins bear a legend on one side with the name of the province: "Judea" (*yəhūd*). Some of the inscriptions also include the personal name and sometimes also title of Judean authorities – information critical for understanding the way the province was administered in the late Persian era and throughout much of the Early Hellenistic period. And the iconography chosen to stamp on these coins, presumably *by* Judeans but certainly *for* Judeans, is crucial for understanding important aspects of Judean cult and culture at this time. The main methodological hurdle involves the dating of these coins to more precise timeframes within the late Persian or Early Hellenistic era, although recent years have seen important advances on this front (see various studies collected in Gitler, Lorber, and Fontanille 2023).

1.4.3 Papyrology

Documents written on papyrus that mention Judeans provide significant information about important aspects of the Judean way of life during the Early Hellenistic period (Tcherikover 1957; Hacham and Ilan 2020). One drawback of these documents is their extraordinarily limited distribution; because papyrus is an organic material (made from the pithy stalks of the papyrus plant), it is only in arid environments like Egypt and the Judean Desert where such documents have survived. Almost all the Early Hellenistic papyri written by or about Judeans were found in Egypt (Figure 3), and therefore their relevance for

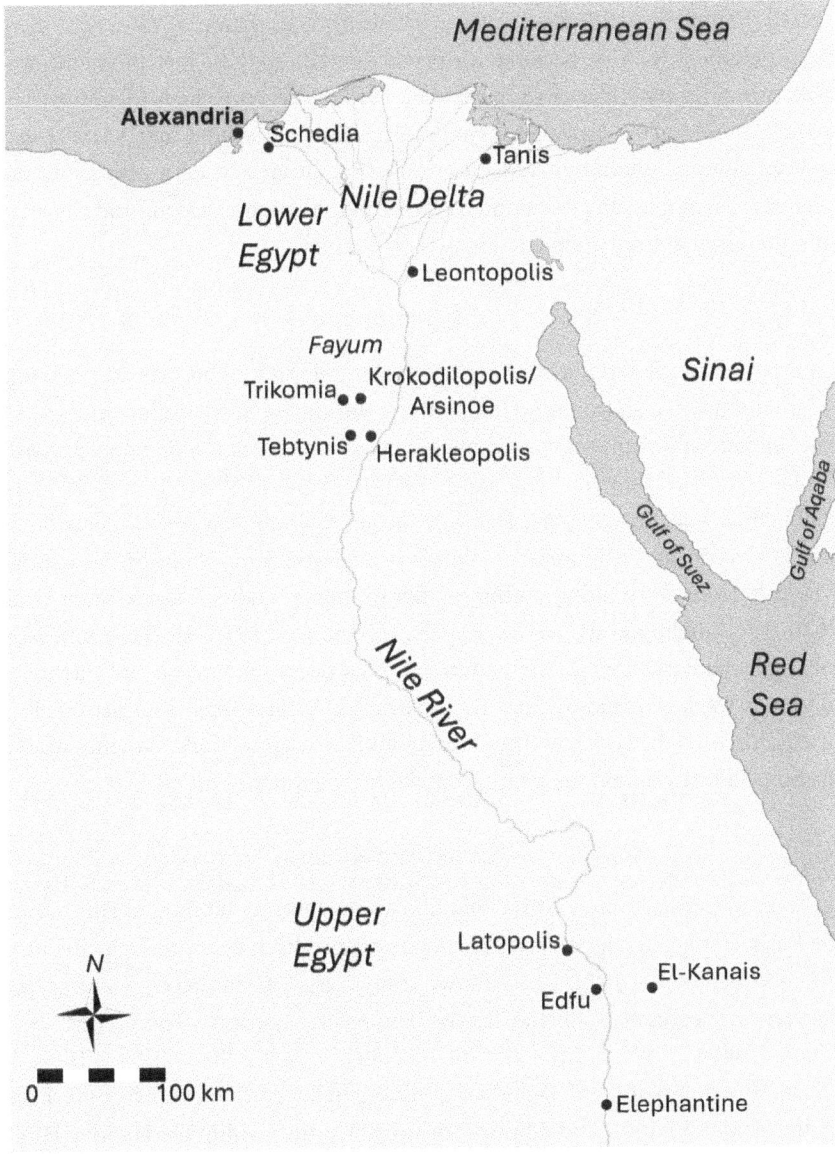

Figure 3 Map of Egypt during the Early Ptolemaic period, indicating locations of Judean communities discussed in this Element (after Hacham and Ilan 2020: 29).

understanding Judean life outside of Egypt is somewhat limited. Another challenge with the use of the papyrological evidence is the problem of determining whether the document in fact mentions Judeans. Unless a person is explicitly identified as a "Judean" within the document, deciding that a document relates to one or more Judeans usually comes down to a decision that a personal name mentioned is a specifically Judean name. Names are usually identified as "Judean" either because they contain a Yahwistic theophoric element, or else because historical sources suggest that the name was used primarily by Judeans (Tcherikover 1957: xvii–xix). Such identifications may be problematic, however, as they often fail to consider that YHWH was revered among certain non-Judean groups (Samaritans being a prime, but not exclusive, example) and that nontheophoric names popular among Judeans may sometimes have been adopted also by non-Judeans.[3]

1.4.4 Epigraphy

Like papyri, texts written on nonperishable materials often provide valuable information about Judeans and their culture during the Early Hellenistic period. This includes inscriptions carved into stone, writing with ink on pottery shards (called ostraca; singular: ostracon), and inscriptions carved into seals or stamped as seal impressions. Because these materials can survive outside of arid environments, epigraphic evidence is available from more of the regions where Judeans were living during the period under study: Judea (Cotton et al. 2010–12; Ameling et al. 2018), Egypt (Tcherikover 1957; Horbury and Noy 1992; Hacham and Ilan 2020), and to a limited degree in Greece and surrounding areas (Noy, Panayotov, and Bloedhorn 2004). However, like papyri, it is often difficult to be sure whether an epigraphic inscription indeed mentions one or more Judeans unless the gentilic "Judean" is explicitly found.

1.4.5 Literary Sources

Another important source of information about Judean culture and cult during the Early Hellenistic period is literary texts penned by Judeans living at the time (Grabbe 2008a: 65–102). The following texts have been dated, with varying degrees of certainty, to the Early Hellenistic period: Tobit, Ben Sira (Ecclesiasticus), early sections of the so-called Enochic literature, the book of Giants, the Aramaic Levi Document, various compositions known only from Qumran, along with scattered texts (or textual strata) within the Hebrew Bible

---

[3] The presence of settlers from Samaria in early Ptolemaic Egypt is suggested by the village name "Samáreia" mentioned in several papyri from this time; see Kuhs (1996).

(see Lange 2006; Grabbe 2008a: 81–84, 94–96, 98–100; Schmid 2021). The third century BCE is thought to mark the start of when Judean scribes began to produce Greek translations of biblical texts (the Septuagint), which may also be regarded as primary sources for the period (Lee 1983; Dorival 1988: 55–58). Also often assigned to this time are fragments from the writings of Demetrius the Chronographer (commonly thought to date to the late third century BCE) and fragments from the writings of Ezekiel the Tragedian and of Artapanus, authors that some scholars also assign to around this time (see Grabbe 2008a: 85–86, 89–92). While these surviving texts almost certainly represent only a small fraction of the entirety of Judean literary output at this time (most of which has since been lost), they are valuable in providing indications about what at least some Judean literati were thinking and writing about during this period.

By definition, all the ancient literary texts mentioned here were the product of intellectuals capable of producing highly sophisticated literature. They are excellent sources for the historian engaged in investigating the *history of ideas*, but they present significant challenges for the scholar who seeks to explore *sociocultural history* on the level of a population at large. The fact that our ancient writers were not only literate but also eminently skilled in composing literature already sets them apart from the Judean masses, most of whom are commonly assumed to have been illiterate. While some of these authors may have been influential elites whose ideas and voices affected the societies within which they were embedded, for the most part we simply do not know if this was the case. It seems just as likely that in many if not most cases, the authors of these ancient texts were little more than fringe figures with limited influence on their surroundings, esoteric intellectuals moving along the outer edges of the societies within which they lived and penned their works. Not only were these ancient texts written by literati who were not *of* the masses, but they were also never written with the intention of providing empirical accounts *about* the behaviors of the masses. The authors of all these texts clearly had other goals in mind, and in fact their writings are for the most part indifferent to what the masses were or were not doing. Where a text *does* refer to behaviors of ordinary Judeans, great care must be exercised to distinguish between the real and the ideal. For the most part, the authors of most of these texts were ideologues harboring quite specific agendas, and their writings must be assessed with this basic fact in mind.

Non-Judean authors who mention Judeans (or who are alleged to have done so) include Theophrastus, Hecataeus of Abdera, Megasthenes, Clearchus of Soli, and Manetho (Stern 1974). In all these cases, these mentions are found in textual fragments preserved only in later literary texts—which often raises questions as to their authenticity and accuracy. And like texts penned by Judeans, literary texts written by non-Judeans are never impartial reports of some objective reality. These are frequently polemical, and the degree to which the authors had genuine familiarity with Judeans of their time is often in question.

The copious writings of Flavius Josephus include narratives set in the Early Hellenistic period, along with citations from documents said to date from this time. As Josephus wrote his works at the end of the first century CE, however, this material can hardly be regarded as primary evidence for the period. Nevertheless, some useful information may still be gleaned from this material when analyzed carefully using critical historical methods (Grabbe 2008a: 74–75).

1.5 Outline of the Element

Following the present introductory section, Section 2 will investigate administrative structures in Judea and among Judean communities in the diaspora, with a special focus on the degree to which power configurations may have either carried over or else shifted from the preceding Persian period. This investigation will lay the groundwork for Section 3, which will explore the degree to which – if at all – Torah law may have been regarded as authoritative and widely observed among the masses during this era. Section 4 will attempt to characterize how and where Judeans performed cultic worship of YHWH, and will explore the degree to which Judeans' devotion to YHWH had by this time become exclusive of reverence paid to other deities. Section 5 will examine the degree to which Judeans had come to adopt elements of Greek culture during this period, paying careful attention to differences over time and between locations. Section 6 will inquire into the literature that might have been well-known and influential within Judean society at large during the Early Hellenistic period. Finally, Section 7 will bring together the analyses from the previous sections, and will attempt to draw more general conclusions regarding whether we ought to regard the Early Hellenistic period largely as one of continuity with the Yahwism of previous eras, or if we should recognize in this period the emergence of a fundamentally novel system we might call Judaism.

2 Administrative Structures

The manner whereby a society is governed impacts directly upon the day-to-day lives of the governed population. As political decisions, policies, and laws can shape a collective's values, beliefs, and behaviors, understanding the ways the group is administered provides crucial context for understanding sociocultural developments within that group. Furthermore, establishing the relationship of a social group toward external power structures can help reveal how open the group may be toward direct or indirect influence from other cultures. And as individuals and institutions wielding power often hold vested interests in matters relating to the cult and culture of the society they rule, shifts in power dynamics often serve as critical catalysts of change in these spheres as well.

Throughout most of the Early Hellenistic period, Judeans everywhere lived under the imperial rule of one Hellenistic regime or another. A fully independent Judean polity would arise only in the Late Hellenistic period, in Judea, following the Maccabean revolt against the Seleucid Kingdom in the middle of the second century BCE. In the present section, we will investigate how Judeans were governed in the era immediately prior to the emergence of this sovereign Judean state, both in their homeland and in their diaspora communities. We will pay special attention here to the ways in which power structures in place under the Achaemenid empire either endured or were altered under Hellenistic rule. This will set the stage for the following section (Section 3), in which we will investigate whether Torah law had come to be adopted as the authoritative legal structure of Judean life already during the Early Hellenistic period.

2.1 Judea

We begin by looking at administrative structures in Judea, beginning with the Persian period, continuing through the early days of Macedonian and Ptolemaic rule, and ending with the shift to Seleucid control at the start of the second century BCE. We will review what evidence survives from throughout this time for a certain degree of autonomy in the administration of Judea through a native Judean governor, high priest, and council of elders, and under a native Judean legal system.

2.1.1 Governor

During the Persian period, the province of Judea (like Samaria and other neighboring provinces) was governed by a local governor called a "*peḥâ*" or "*paḥwā*" in Aramaic. A letter on papyrus sent from the Judean community on Elephantine, dated to 407 BCE and preserved in two copies, was addressed directly to one such governor, named Bagohi (*TAD*, A4.7:1, A4.8:1). In this letter, the Elephantine Judeans requested that the governor of Judea intercede on behalf of the rebuilding of the Judean temple on Elephantine, which had been destroyed three years previously by Egyptian troops and priests. The letter concludes with a note claiming that a similar request had been sent also to "Delaiah and Shelemiah, the sons of Sanballat the governor of Samaria" (*TAD*, A4.7:29, A4.8:28). Fortuitously, an undated memorandum recording the joint reply of Bagohi and Delaiah in support of the rebuilding of the temple has also survived (*TAD*, A4.9). Together, these documents provide valuable information about the power the Judean governor wielded well beyond the borders of the province itself, and the relationship this governor had fostered with at least one Judean community in the diaspora.

Probably from around the same time (the late sixth through early fourth centuries BCE), the title "governor" appears also on stamped jar handles found in Judea itself – some of which also bear the name of the province ("*yəhûd*") (Lipschits and Vanderhooft 2011: 77–106, 192–201, 235–52). The stamped jars were likely used to collect taxes in the form of produce (wine and oil) for delivery to the provincial authorities, headed by the provincial governor (Lipschits and Vanderhooft 2011: 758–64). It seems likely that at least some of these governors were themselves Judean, since at least two of the personal names bearing this title on these stamps are Hebrew – " '*ăḥîāv*" and "*yəhô 'ezer*" (*YSI*, types 1 and 7) – and the latter is clearly Yahwistic. Possibly also from around this time are two bullae (unprovenanced) with seal impressions mentioning " '*elnātān* the governor," likely another Judean name (Avigad 1976: 5–7, 11–13). The sum of this epigraphic evidence suggests that there was likely some historical accuracy to the way that Hebrew Bible narratives set in Persian-era Judea depict a province largely governed on the local level by a Judean governor ("*peḥâ*") appointed by Achaemenid royal authority (e.g., Hag 1–2; Neh 5:14; 12:26) (see Grabbe 2004: 148–149).

One of the silver coin types bearing the name of the province of Judea also bears the name of its governor: "*yəḥizqiyyâ* the governor" (*happeḥâ*) (*YC*, type 24) – clearly a Hebrew, Yahwistic name (Figure 4). Although originally dated to the late Persian period (Meshorer 2001: 15–16), this coin is now thought to date

Figure 4 Silver coin bearing the Paleo-Hebrew legend "*yəḥizqiyyâ* the governor (*happeḥâ*)" (*YC*, type 24); pre-Ptolemaic Macedonian period (Photo © The Israel Museum, Jerusalem).

to the period following the conquests of Alexander the Great, but before the start of Ptolemaic rule over Judea (Gitler, Lorber, and Fontanille 2023: 115–18). If this new dating is correct, it would suggest that the office of governor – still filled by a Judean – continued to hold authority over Judea for some time after the Macedonian conquests.

The legend on this coin appears to be the latest surviving evidence for the existence of any sort of provincial governor holding executive authority locally over Judea. The title (or one like it) does not appear on coins, stamped handles, in documentary papyri, or in literary texts written during or about the Ptolemaic period. Once we reach the Seleucid period, we encounter a certain Ptolemy son of Thraseas who served under Antiochus III as the "military governor (*stratagòs* [sic]) and high priest of Coele-Syria and Phoenicia" following the Seleucid king's conquest of this region at the turn of the second century BCE (*OGIS*, no. 230). The province of "Coele-Syria and Phoenicia" encompassed a large area of the Levant that included the smaller region of Judea. A stone stele containing a dossier of ten correspondences between this Ptolemy and Antiochus was found near Kibbutz Heftziba, west of Beth She'an (Heinrichs 2018). And Josephus quoted in full a letter he alleges was sent by Antiochus to this Ptolemy, commanding him with detailed instructions about the administration of Judea and the city of Jerusalem (Josephus, *Ant.* 12.138–44). None of these documents mention anything about a provincial governor of Judea who would have been subordinate to Ptolemy, which may suggest that no such office existed by this time.

Regardless of the ultimate fate of the governor's office itself, it is important to point out that the practice of stamping jar handles for administrative purposes continued uninterrupted throughout the Early Hellenistic period and even into the beginning of the Late Hellenistic period (Lipschits and Vanderhooft 2011). This phenomenon, whose roots may be traced as far back as the late eighth century BCE, reflects a strikingly conservative feature of Judean administrative traditions over the course of some six centuries that Judea was subjugated under the great empires of Assyria, Egypt, Babylonia, and Persia, followed by the Ptolemaic and Seleucid Kingdoms. It was only after the Hasmoneans reestablished Judean sovereignty that the system disappeared, signalling a stark break in the structures which administered Judea (Lipschits 2021).

2.1.2 High Priest

In the Elephantine letter from 407 BCE cited previously, the writers mention that they had previously sent a petition on the same matter to both the governor of Judea and to "*yəhôḥānān* the high priest and his colleagues, the priests who are in Jerusalem" (*TAD*, A4.7:18; see also A4.8:17). As the high priest of Jerusalem was being petitioned to assist in the restoration of the Yahwistic temple at Elephantine, clearly the high priest at the end of the fifth century BCE was regarded as an authority who wielded some amount of power even beyond the province of Judea—at least with regard to matters of cult. And the fact that the earlier letter is said to have been addressed not only to the high priest but also to "his colleagues, the priests who are in Jerusalem" suggests that the high priest of the time was situated at the top of a hierarchy of priests, which as a body appears to have held an important position of authority. Further references to the high priesthood during the Persian period may be found in literary sources, primarily the Hebrew Bible and the works of Josephus, but it is difficult to extract historically accurate information from any of these texts (see Grabbe 2004: 147–48, 230–34).

Among the silver coins minted in Judea is a type bearing the legend "*yôḥānyâ* the priest" (*hakkôhēn*) (*YC*, type 25), likely meaning the *high* priest (Figure 5). Although originally dated to the late Persian period (and the personal name misread as "*yôḥānān*": Meshorer 2001: 14), this coin is now thought to date to the period following the conquests of Alexander the Great, but before the beginning of Ptolemaic rule over Judea (Gitler, Lorber, and Fontanille 2023: 117). If this new dating is correct, it would suggest that the office of high priest continued to hold a position of authority for some time after the Macedonian conquests. And the fact that at this time coins were being minted under the auspices not only of the governor but also of the high priest suggests that the office entailed some amount of authority beyond the immediate sphere of the temple and its cult.

Figure 5 Silver coin bearing the Paleo-Hebrew legend "*yôḥānyâ* the priest (*hakkôhēn*)" (*YC*, type 25); pre-Ptolemaic Macedonian period (Photo © The Israel Museum, Jerusalem).

No inscriptional evidence mentioning a high priest in Jerusalem has survived from the time of Ptolemaic or Seleucid rule over Judea, whether in documentary papyri, on coins, or on epigraphic remains. After a gap in the inscriptional record of around two hundred years, we once again find mention of a "high priest" on the coins of John Hyrcanus I (134–104 BCE) (*TJC*, Groups A–J). The only evidence we have for the high priesthood during the Ptolemaic and early Seleucid periods comes from literary sources, most of which were written many years after the time they purport to describe.[4] The account presented in the Letter of Aristeas, for example, is set during the reign of Ptolemy II Philadelphus (reigned 285–246 BCE) and features a high priest named Eleazar. Although presented as an eyewitness report, the story is almost unanimously regarded by scholars as a fiction written at least a century after the events it purports to describe (White, Keddie, and Flexsenhar 2018: 34–38). And in the writings of Josephus, especially in book 12 of his *Antiquities*, we find names and stories about several high priests who are said to have held office during the course of the Early Hellenistic era. But as Josephus wrote toward the end of the first century CE, this material too is highly problematic for extracting accurate historical information (see Grabbe 2008a: 225–29). The only text with an extensive depiction of a high priest and his responsibilities which may be dated with any degree of confidence to the period under discussion is Ben Sira 50:1–21, probably from the first quarter of the second century BCE. Here, the author gives praise to the high priest Simon, son of Onias, who is said to have engaged in repairing and fortifying the temple, constructing a reservoir, and fortifying the city of Jerusalem against siege. This text suggests that by the end of the Early Hellenistic period, it made sense for an author to depict the high priest holding significant authority outside the direct sphere of the temple cult, such as overseeing massive construction projects.

The basic autonomy of the Judean high priest from the oversight of the Seleucid authorities in the early second century BCE may be inferred from a royal inscription unearthed at Maresha and dated 178 BCE (*CIIP*, no. 3511) (Figure 6). In it is preserved an order sent by Seleucus IV to his chief official, Heliodorus, instructing him regarding the administration of the temples in the region of Coele-Syria and Phoenicia – which included Judea.[5] After noting the current state of affairs in which the region's temples lacked direct oversight by

---

[4] Scholars often regard a depiction of the Judean high priesthood given by the mid first-century BCE author Diodorus Siculus as an accurate quotation from the writings of the Hecataeus of Abdera (ca. 300), but this is unfounded (see Section 3.2.1).

[5] Fragments from two additional, almost identical copies of this order have been discovered: one is reported to have been found at Maresha (*CIIP*, no. 3512), and one was unearthed at Byblos (Yon 2015).

20   *The Archaeology of Ancient Israel*

Figure 6 Limestone stele from Maresha (in Idumea) containing order in Greek from Seleucus IV Philopator concerning Olympiodorus (*CIIP*, no. 3511); 178 BCE (Photo © The Israel Museum, Jerusalem, by Elie Posner).

the Seleucid authorities, Seleucus directs Heliodorus to appoint a certain Olympiodorus to fill this role: "as the affairs in Coele-Syria and Phoenicia are lacking someone in charge for their (i.e., the sanctuaries') care, we observed that Olympiodorus will preside prudently over their orderly conduct" (*CIIP*, no. 3511:23–27). It seems reasonable to infer from here that the until this time, the priestly officials governing the region's temples – including the high priest of the Jerusalem temple – would have enjoyed a substantial degree of independence from any meddling of Seleucid bureaucrats.[6] It seems plausible that such a state of affairs might have been in place already in the third century BCE, under the previous Ptolemaic regime.

In summary, while it does seem likely that the high priesthood remained an important office throughout the Early Hellenistic period, it remains difficult to characterize precisely what kind of authority a high priest during this time might have held. Whatever his powers were, ultimately the Judean high priest would have been subordinate to more powerful authorities within the Hellenistic imperial courts.

2.1.3 Governing Council

In the previously discussed papyrus from Elephantine, the writers mention a group of "Judean nobles" ("*ḥōrê yəhûdāyē*") as the addressees of an earlier-sent petition alongside the governor of Judea, the high priest and his priestly colleagues – all of whom are appealed to as holders of power (*TAD*, A4.7:19; see also A4.8:18). Precisely how these noblemen might have played a role in the administration of Judea, and whether they served on some sort of formally convoked council, remains essentially unknown (Grabbe 2004: 154–55; 234–35).

Meager but tantalizing evidence has survived for the possible existence of a council of elders governing in Judea during the Early Hellenistic period. As mentioned earlier, Josephus cited a letter allegedly sent by Antiochus III to his military governor, Ptolemy, following the Seleucid conquest of Judea. The letter opens with a description of the warm welcome the king and his army received upon his arrival in Jerusalem, including a formal reception by the city's "council of elders" (*tẽs gerousías*) (Josephus, *Ant.* 12:138). In return for this honor, the king granted this council exemptions from certain taxes (Josephus, *Ant.* 12:142). If scholarly consensus is correct in accepting Josephus' text as an authentic and accurately cited document from the turn of the second century BCE (e.g., Bickerman 2007a; Grabbe 2008a: 324–26), we would have evidence for the existence of some sort of Judean council of elders governing locally in Jerusalem during late Ptolemaic and early Seleucid

---

[6] The order of Seleucus here is probably the historical backdrop to the legend recorded in 2 Macc 3 (and likely hinted at in Dan 11:20) regarding the failed attempt of Heliodorus to rob the Jerusalem temple; see Gera 2009: 148–49.

rule (Grabbe 2008a: 230–31).[7] How such a body might have been convened and what their powers would have included, however, remain essentially unknown (Bickerman 2007a: 319).

2.1.4 Native Legal System

In Ezra 7:12–26, we encounter an Aramaic text presented as an official letter given to Ezra the Scribe by a Persian king Artaxerxes, in which Ezra is instructed to appoint local "magistrates and judges" in Judea to enforce the laws of the Judean god upon all denizens of the province. As no primary evidence dating to the Persian period that might corroborate the biblical claims on the matter has survived, we cannot know whether at this time the province was truly governed according to native Judean laws adjudicated by local judges.

In a letter which Josephus alleges was sent by Antiochus III to Ptolemy his governor circa 200 BCE, the Seleucid king instructs: "All who belong to the people are to be governed in accordance with their ancestral laws [*politeuésthōsan dè pántes hoi ek toũ éthnous katà toùs patríous nómous*]" (Josephus, *Ant.* 12:142). E. Bickerman, who regarded this letter as authentic, described this document as the "Seleucid charter for Jerusalem" – an ordinance which reestablished the municipal statutes which had previously been in place under Ptolemaic rule, immediately prior to his conquest (Bickerman 2007a). If so, this would suggest that Judea was governed by its own system of laws by the late Ptolemaic period, and that this arrangement was continued under early Seleucid rule. (See Section 3.2.3, where we will explore whether the "ancestral laws" here should be identified with the Torah.)

2.2 The Judean Diaspora

Earlier generations of scholars commonly entertained the hypothesis that Judean communities in the Greco-Roman diaspora were often organized according to the model of a civic body called a *políteuma* (plural: *politeúmata*). While the term carries a variety of meanings in the Greek sources, the model usually cited was of a distinct ethnic group, originally alien to the city within which it had settled, and which came to be recognized by officials in the host city as a semi-autonomous community with its own constitution and with its own officials administering its internal affairs (Kasher 2002: 258–60). The understanding was that this was a standard model of ethnic self-governance in Greek cities throughout the Hellenistic world, and was implemented by Judeans in much the same way that

---

[7] Probably from around this same time, Ben Sira provides further possible allusions to such a council (Sir 7:14; 38:32–33), but these are too unclear to allow us to draw any compelling historical conclusions.

it was by other ethnic groups residing in Greek cities, such as Idumeans, Lykians, and others (Tcherikover 1957: 6, 1959: 299–305).

This hypothesis came under a barrage of critique starting in the late 1980s and continuing through the 1990s (Zuckerman 1988, followed by studies listed in Kasher 2002: 260n10). First, it was pointed out that the term never appears among the surviving assemblage of Judean documentary papyri from Egypt, nor (with one questionable exception) does it ever appear within literary sources like Philo and Josephus, which often provide detailed accounts about Judean communities in the diaspora (Zuckerman 1988: 171–74). Furthermore, scholars began to question whether the term *políteuma* as it was found among other ethnic groups ever referred to a civic body with political, administrative rights. Instead, it was argued that *politeúmata* were associations of foreigners who formed for various purposes, like burial societies, professional associations, or to facilitate social or cultic functions unique to the group (Zuckerman 1988: 174–80).

The 2001 publication of a papyri archive from Herakleopolis (in Middle Egypt) provided the first documentary evidence of a Judean community organized as a self-governing *políteuma* (Cowey and Maresch 2001, republished together with an additional document in *CPJ* 4, nos. 557–77). The cache is composed of twenty-one documents dated to the short timespan 144/3–133/2 BCE. From the documents we learn that the Judean *políteuma* was governed by a collective body of officials called *árkhontes* (plural of *árkhōn*), directed by a governor called the *politárkhēs* (Cowey and Maresch 2001: 10–18). Judges (*kritaí*) and a court of law (*kritḗrion*) are also mentioned in the documents. The authority of the *políteuma* clearly extended beyond Herakleopolis, as in some petitions (*CPJ* 4, nos. 562, 564, 565, 569), either one or both of the parties to the dispute were residents of villages or towns outside the city (Cowey and Maresch 2001: 18–23). Members of the *políteuma*, all men, are designated as "citizens" (*polĩtai*), while nonmembers are called "strangers" (*allóphuloi*). Judean representatives of the *políteuma* outside Herakleopolis itself are referred to as "elders" (*presbúteroi*). Most of the documents are petitions made by private citizens to the *árkhontes*, and some are petitions made directly to the *politárkhēs*. The petitions concern such matters as a marriage contract (*CPJ* 4, no. 559), the dissolution of a betrothal (*CPJ* 4, no. 560), a loan (*CPJ* 4, no. 564) and a debt (*CPJ* 4, no. 567), an unpaid lease (*CPJ* 4, no. 568), the purchase of a slave and a wet-nursing contract (*CPJ* 4, no. 565), a complaint about nondelivery of ordered wool (*CPJ* 4, no. 566), and the release of a prisoner (*CPJ* 4, no. 558). While it is not known what system of law might have been used to adjudicate these cases, the (albeit somewhat late) documents tantalizingly refer to such concepts as an "ancestral oath" (*hórkou patríou*) (*CPJ* 4, nos. 558:28–29; 565:7–8; 568:10) and "the ancestral law" (*tòn pátrion nómon*) (*CPJ* 4, no. 560:28–29).

Clearly, this specific Judean community enjoyed a certain degree of self-governance according to the model of a semi-autonomous *políteuma*, and some neighboring Judean communities appear to have been subject to its jurisdiction. A question that looms large, however, is just how common such Judean *políteumata* might have been in other cities throughout the rest of the Hellenistic diaspora. The clear evidence that such a communal structure did exist at Herakleopolis lends support to the possible existence of a Judean *políteuma* in Alexandria, as suggested by some literary sources (e.g., Let. Aris. 310; Josephus, *Ant.* 14:116–17). Two honorary inscriptions from Berenike in Cyrenaica mentioning a Judean *políteuma* from the Augustan period (*CJZC*, nos. 70–71) suggest that the model might have existed outside of Egypt as well. And the possibility that at least some Judean communities in the Seleucid diaspora might have also enjoyed a degree of autonomy is suggested by a document Josephus alleges was sent by Antiochus III to the governor of Lydia, in which he ordered the transportation of two thousand Judean families from Babylonia to Phrygia, where they are to be allowed to "use their own laws [*nómois autoùs khrēsthai toĩs idíois*]" (Josephus *Ant.* 12:150). It must be stressed that the entirety of this evidence dates to the second century BCE and later, and accordingly whether any Judean communities in the Hellenistic diaspora of the third century BCE or earlier may have enjoyed any kind of semi-autonomous governance of the sort discussed here remains essentially a matter of speculation.

2.3 Conclusions

We have reviewed here limited but instructive evidence relating to administrative structures in place for governing both the province of Judea as well as individual Judean communities scattered throughout the reigning Hellenistic kingdoms. These data seem to suggest that during the Early Hellenistic period, Judeans enjoyed a certain degree of semiautonomous authority both in Judea itself and probably also abroad – much like in the preceding Persian period. If, as it seems, the power structures governing Judeans reflect a significant degree of continuity from Achaemenid times through the Early Hellenistic period, any sociocultural developments that might have occurred during this time can hardly be pinned on substantial shifts in structural power dynamics. The stability of the semiautonomous governance under which Judeans appear to have lived would have allowed the maintenance of stable cultural and cultic structures, at least up until the outbreak of the Maccabean revolt and the emergence of the Hasmoneans' revolutionary new regime.

The evidence we have seen for the use of Judean "ancestral laws" in Judea (as cited by Josephus) and in the diaspora (as cited in the somewhat late Herakleopolis archive) raises the question of what exactly might have been meant by the term if it was indeed used at this early stage. When the "ancestral laws" are spoken of in first-century CE sources like Philo and Josephus, in most cases there can be little doubt that the laws of the Torah are meant. For the Early Hellenistic period, however, this cannot simply be assumed, as many scholars often do (e.g., Tcherikover 1957: 7, 1959: 305–6; Bickerman 2007a: 355). We will investigate this question in detail in the next section.

3 Torah Law

At some stage, the Judean way of life came to be governed by a system of rules and regulations known as the "Torah." The term derives from the Hebrew "*tôrâ*," a noun that appears more than two hundred times in the Hebrew Bible and carries a meaning approximating "instruction" or "teaching." Eventually, the word came to refer to a very specific text – the Pentateuch – which was regarded as the quintessential body of divine instruction given to Israel through Moses. And later, the term took on the additional sense of the entire system of law that had developed surrounding the Pentateuch and through its dynamic interpretation. The term Torah as it will be used here will refer to this latter, expansive understanding of the term.

In the present section, we will explore the question of whether in the Early Hellenistic period, ordinary Judeans knew about and observed the laws of the Torah both in their daily lives and on a communal level. The question is not if the *notion* of a Mosaic Torah existed as an *ideal* in the minds of Judean ideologues, thinkers, and writers. Rather, our concern will be whether the rules and regulations of the Torah were widely known, regarded as authoritative, and put into *practice* by the masses of ordinary Judeans on a societal level.

We begin by examining whether Early Hellenistic archaeological and inscriptional evidence from Judea and Egypt provides any indication of widespread Torah observance at this time. This will be followed by an examination of literary sources which have been interpreted in the past as indicating that the Torah was widely regarded as authoritative already in the Early Hellenistic period.

3.1 Archaeological and Inscriptional Evidence

3.1.1 Judea

An abundance of material evidence pointing to widespread observance of the Torah has survived from Hasmonean and Herodian period Judea. This includes over a thousand ritual immersion pools unearthed throughout the

Southern Levant which were used to fulfill the bathing requirements mandated by the ritual purity rules of the Torah (Adler 2022: 61–66, 82–83). Also attesting to widespread observance of the Torah's purity laws is the widespread distribution of tableware and storage vessels fashioned from chalk, as stone came to be regarded as a raw material impervious to ritual impurity (Adler 2022: 66–71, 83–84). Figural art depicting humans or animals was almost entirely absent from the artistic repertoire of Judea at the time, clearly in deference to a strict understanding of the "second commandment," which proscribed the making of graven images (Adler 2022: 92–101, 102–6). This is particularly striking in the coinage of these periods, as figural art – and especially portraits of the ruling authority – were ubiquitous on coins practically everywhere else throughout the Greco-Roman world. Widespread observance of the Torah's dietary restrictions is supported by a lack of pig and scaleless fish bones in zooarchaeological assemblages from Judean settlement sites (Adler 2022: 31–37, 43, 46). Among the discoveries in the Judean Desert caves from these periods are dozens of tefillin and mezuzot, ritual artifacts used to fulfill a literalist interpretation of verses in Exodus (13:9, 16) and Deuteronomy (6:8–9, 11:18, 20) (Adler 2022: 118–26, 129–30). The ritual of taking four species on the festival of Sukkot (Lev 23:40) is depicted on coins (Adler 2022: 159). And the Pentateuchal commandment to ceremonially light a seven-branched candelabrum in the sanctum is depicted in Judean art and on coins from this time (Adler 2022: 164–65).

The entirety of this substantial body of evidence dates to the middle of the second century BCE and onward. Strikingly, no archaeological or inscriptional remains indicative of Torah observance are known from the Early Hellenistic period. While this lack of evidence is quite unambiguous, it should not be interpreted *necessarily* as evidence of absence. One might easily hypothesize that at this time, Judeans were observing the Torah in ways that left no imprint on the material record. Perhaps the ritual bathing mandated by the Torah took place without artificially constructed immersion pools, and perhaps the ritual purity regulations surrounding food were observed without depending on the convenience of stone vessels. It is easy to imagine that prior to the Hasmonean period, the "second commandment" was observed not through wholesale avoidance of figural art, but by avoiding the fashioning of cultic images worshiped as deities. As only a small quantity of zooarchaeological remains from Judea is dated with any precision to the Early Hellenistic period, we cannot draw any substantial conclusions from these finds about Judeans' adherence to the dietary laws at this time. One can easily hypothesize that it was only in the Hasmonean period that literalist interpretations gave rise to the tefillin and mezuzot rituals, whereas in earlier periods, the relevant Pentateuchal instructions were observed in ways which left no material remains. And perhaps the ritual of the four species on Sukkot was observed and the seven-branched menorah was lit in the temple, without anyone feeling the need to depict these observances in coins or on other forms of artwork. Finally, a lack of finds indicative of Torah observance in the Early Hellenistic period may simply be a result of the general difficulty in dating archaeological levels to this timeframe, as noted in the introductory section (Section 1.4.1).

Having registered these important reservations about drawing undue conclusions on the basis of an absence of evidence, we will note here certain limited indications of *negative* evidence – data which suggests that certain Torah regulations were *not* being adhered to. In the following section (Section 4.2), we will examine evidence that suggests that at least some Judeans at this time paid reverence to deities other than YHWH – a phenomenon which is quite difficult to square with any reasonable interpretation of Torah observance. As we shall see there, intimations of this are found on circulating coins minted by a Judean governor and a Judean high priest, which suggests that the phenomenon was less than fringe. We might also mention here that the only published fish remains from an Early Hellenistic level in Judea includes some bones from scaleless fish. As the size of this assemblage (sixteen identified specimens, of which three are catfish) is very small, however, no significant conclusions should be drawn from these finds (Adler and Lernau 2021: 16n14).

3.1.2 Egypt

A somewhat enigmatic reference to the Sabbath appears among the Egyptian papyri, in a document thought to date to around the time of Ptolemy II Philadelphus in the middle of the third century BCE (*CPJ* 1, no. 10). The papyrus contains an account of bricks received by the unnamed writer of the document, which were delivered to him by a certain Phileas, a certain Demetrios, and unknown persons from Tanis. The account provides the number of bricks delivered from the fifth to the eleventh of the Egyptian month of Epeiph (no year is cited), but on the seventh of the month – instead of writing a sum of bricks – the author of the account wrote only "*Sábbata*" (Sabbath). It seems that either the one who delivered the bricks, the one who received the bricks, or else the bricklayers for whom the bricks were intended took vacation from work on "Sabbaths." Whether or not those involved (presumably Judeans) would have regarded work on the Sabbath to have been *forbidden* by dint of something like Torah law is difficult to know from this singular document. Several scholars have posited that originally – prior to the promulgation of the Pentateuch as Torah – the "Sabbath" was a monthly festival celebrated on the full moon, and not characterized by any specific prohibitions against work (Meinhold 1909; Robinson 1988). It seems possible that the term "*Sábbata*" in our papyrus refers to just such a traditional Judean holiday, when Judean workers would have taken a break from their normal labors as others would have on their customary holidays. If so, this text should not be taken as an indication that Judeans necessarily knew and observed the Torah as early as the third century BCE.

Documentary papyri provide evidence that at least some Judeans at this time were *not* adhering to the Pentateuchal prohibition against charging of interest on a loan (Exod 22:24; Lev 25:35–37; Deut 23:20–21). A loan deed from Tebtynis (in the Fayum), dated to 228–221 BCE, records a loan between two individuals identified as Judeans, which bore interest at a rate of approximately 2 percent per month (*CPJ* 1, no. 20). Another loan contract, from Trikomia (also in the Fayum) and dated to 174 BCE, records a loan between two Judeans that also bore a 2 percent interest rate per month (*CPJ* 1, no. 24) (Figure 7). And from slightly later, a petition to the Judean *árkhontes* of Herakleopolis dated to 133 BCE tells of a loan between Judeans that bore an identical interest rate of 2 percent per month (*CPJ* 4, no. 564). This latter document is significant in that it suggests that the Judean petitioner had no qualms about bringing his petition before the official Judean body for adjudication, despite its wanton disregard for the Torah prohibition against interest (Hacham and Ilan 2020: 111).[8]

3.2 Literary Evidence

Some scholars have interpreted certain literary sources thought to have been penned during the Early Hellenistic period as indicating that the Torah was widely

---

[8] It bears briefly discussing here another Late Hellenistic papyrus (dated to 134 BCE) from the same archive of Herakleopolis. A man petitioned to the Judean *árkhontes* claiming that he "was betrothed (*emnēsteusámēn*)" to a woman through oaths made "according to the law (*katà tòn nómon*)," but which were subsequently abrogated without provision of "the customary divorce deed (*tò eithisménon toũ apostasíou tò bublíon*)" (*CPJ* 4, no. 560). Several scholars have posited that this papyrus is predicated on the laws of the Torah surrounding betrothal and divorce (see bibliography cited in Hacham and Ilan 2020: 98). They stake this claim on the fact that the legal notion of a binding betrothal whose abrogation necessitates the granting of a formal divorce document is a uniquely Judean one, unknown from Greek law. The reliance of the author of this papyrus on the Torah is further supported by his use of the same term for "betrothal" as is found in the Septuagint translation of Deut 22:23–29 (Hebrew: "*məʾōrāśâ ləʾîš*"; Greek: "*memnēsteuménē andrì*") and for a "divorce deed" in the Septuagint translation of Deut 24:1–4 (Hebrew: "*sēfer kərîtūt*"; Greek: "*biblíon apostasíou*"). None of this, however, necessitates that the scribe who penned the papyrus in question knew of Deuteronomy, whether in the original or in the Greek. Deuteronomy itself seems to reflect – rather than prescribe – ancient Israelite/Judean customs surrounding betrothal and divorce. Until Deuteronomy became widely accepted as authoritative Torah, these early customs likely continued to be practiced independently from any Pentateuchal prooftext (for other examples of this phenomenon, see Adler 2025). The Greek terms used for these practices among Greek-speaking Judeans are reflected in both the Septuagint and in our papyrus document, without the latter *necessarily* being dependent on the former.

Figure 7 Papyrus from Trikomia (in the Fayum, Egypt) with loan contract in Greek recording an interest-bearing loan between two Judeans (*CPJ* 1, no. 24); 174 BCE (=*P.Tebt.* III.1 818. Photo: Courtesy of the Center for the Tebtunis Papyri, University of California, Berkeley).

regarded as authoritative by this time. We will examine here the most important of these sources: citations purportedly from Hecataeus of Abdera, the Septuagint, two letters and a "proclamation" allegedly issued by Antiochus III, and Ben Sira.

3.2.1 Hecataeus of Abdera

Some scholars have argued that an alleged citation from Hecataeus of Abdera demonstrates that the Torah had come to be widely known and observed among ordinary Judeans by the turn of the third century BCE (e.g., Albertz 2001: 40–45; Grabbe 2001b: 98–99). I will argue here that the text in question dates to a time significantly later than 300 BCE, and accordingly contributes nothing toward answering the question of widespread Torah observance at this early date.[9]

Photius, the ninth-century CE Byzantine Patriarch of Constantinople, cited in his *Bibliotheca* (Cod. 244) a text we are told derives from a now lost book of the mid-first-century BCE author Diodorus Siculus (*Bibliotheca Historica* 40.3). In this citation, Diodorus prefaces his report about Pompey's war against the Judeans in the 60s BCE with a brief historical overview of "both the foundation of this nation from the beginning, and the customs [*nómima*] among them."[10] Diodorus goes on to tell about how the Judeans originated as aliens living in Egypt, and after having been driven out of the country, went on to establish a colony in Judea and a city in Jerusalem under the leadership of Moses. This Moses is said to have "established the offices and rites for the divinity, codified and arranged the things relating to the constitution [*tà katà tḕn politeían enomothétēsé te kaì diétaxe*].... He established sacrifices and modes of conduct for everyday life [*tàs katà tòn bíon agōgás*] differing from those of other nations." The priests, headed by a high priest, are said to have been entrusted with guardianship over this "constitution," while the Judean masses are said to show complete obedience to the priestly interpretations of these laws. Diodorus concludes with the following remark: "But during the [foreign] rules that happened later, out of mingling with men of other nations —both under the hegemony of the Persians and of the Macedonians who overthrew this [hegemony]—many of the traditional customs of the Judeans [*tõn patríōn toîs Ioudaíois nomímōn*] were distorted."

Photius himself rejected this account presented by Diodorus as a distortion, adding that Diodorus falsely claimed that his knowledge about the Judeans was indebted to the work of Hecataeus of Miletus: "Using a cunning device as a refuge for himself, he attributes to another [author] the above said things, which are contrary to history. For he [i.e., Diodorus] adds: 'As concerns the Judeans, this is what Hecataeus of Miletus relates about the Judeans.'" Today, most scholars reject Photius's skepticism regarding Diodorus's assertion that

---

[9] We will not discuss here a separate citation which Josephus attributed to Hecataeus (*Ag. Ap.* 1:183–204), as this is widely rejected by modern scholars as pseudepigraphic and as having been written by a Judean at a much later time; see Bar-Kochva 1996.

[10] All translations here follow Bar-Kochva 2010: 100–3.

he had gleaned his knowledge about the Judeans from an earlier Hecataeus (e.g., Bar-Kochva 1996: 18–43; 2010: 90–135; Grabbe 2008b; Collins 2024). However, not only do these scholars believe that Diodorus truly was informed by this earlier work – they have gone one step further in asserting that almost the entire citation from the work of Diodorus presented to us by Photius is actually *a direct citation* from Hecataeus! Additionally, most scholars have emended the word "*Milésios*" with "*Abdērítēs*," arguing that Diodorus would have most likely meant Hecataeus of Abdera (ca. 300 BCE) rather than the earlier Hecataeus of Miletus (ca. 500 BCE) (Bar-Kochva 2010: 105–6n43).

Even if we were to assume that Diodorus had an authentic work of Hecataeus of Abdera from which he learned his information about the Judeans, there seems to be little reason to think that Diodorus's account represents a *direct citation* from Hecataeus (Kratz 2021: 270–74; Adler 2022: 209–11). Indeed, from what Photius tells us, Diodorus does not seem to have ever made any such claim. According to Photius, Diodorus simply informed his readers from whence he had gleaned his knowledge about Judeans. There seems to be little reason to assume that Diodorus would have been informed *only* from the alleged work of Hecataeus and not from any later sources of information. And certainly, there seems to be little reason to assume that Diodorus' words comprise anything resembling a *direct citation* from Hecataeus. To the contrary, Diodorus is known to have regularly drawn from several sources, which he then mingled to produce his own historical constructions (Burton 1972: 34; Berthelot 2008: 5n19). Accordingly, we should regard what appears to be a description of widespread Torah observance among ordinary Judeans in Photius' citation from Diodorus not as an account from the time of Hecataeus, but rather as a reflection of much later realities in the first century BCE.[11]

3.2.2 The Septuagint

The Letter of Aristeas tells a tale of how Ptolemy II Philadelphus (285–246 BCE) recruited a group of seventy-two Judean elders from Jerusalem, bringing them to Alexandria in order to translate the Judean law into Greek. While scholars today almost unanimously agree that this story is largely fictional, many regard an Alexandrian provenance and a third century BCE date as likely for the initial production of what we know of as the Septuagint translation of the Pentateuch (Lee 1983; Dorival 1988: 55–58).

Several speculative explanations have been proposed for *why* the initiative was taken to translate the Pentateuch into Greek in third-century BCE

---

[11] For the possibility that Diodorus drew from a "Pseudo-Hecataeus" penned by a Hasmonean-period Judean author, see Schwartz 2003.

Alexandria (Dorival 1988: 66–78). Most scholars have rejected the explanation given in the Letter of Aristeas, according to which the initiative came from Ptolemy's chief librarian, Demetrius of Phalerum, in order to help complete the royal library in Alexandria (Let. Aris. 9–11). Instead, some have argued that the initiative came from the Judean community of Alexandria, out of liturgical or educational needs of a community that was no longer proficient in Hebrew (Dorival 1988: 67–71). Others have argued that it was a state initiative, intended to provide a legal framework for the Judean communities living within the Ptolemaic realm (Dorival 1988: 72–73; Mélèze-Modrzejewski 1996, 2001).[12]

All these explanations rest on the assumption that by the third century BCE, the Pentateuch was already regarded by the Judean community in Alexandria as in some way authoritative, and perhaps even served as the basis for structuring the community's legal system. It is precisely this assumption, however, that we seek to interrogate here. Certainly, one might imagine an initiative to translate the Pentateuch for entirely scholastic reasons, without the text having already attained widespread acceptance as authoritative Torah. As noted previously, the Letter of Aristeas portrays just such a scenario, where the non-Judean librarian of the royal library in Alexandria initiated and commissioned the translation. Alternatively, one might imagine the initiative coming from Judean intellectuals. Regardless, the very fact that the Pentateuch had been translated into Greek cannot be taken as a necessary indication that by this time ordinary Judeans had already adopted the Pentateuch as the foundational text of a prescriptive and authoritative Torah law.

3.2.3 The Letters and Proclamation of Antiochus III

In the previous section (Section 2.1.3), I cited a letter Josephus alleges was sent by Antiochus III circa 200 BCE to his military governor, Ptolemy, commanding him with detailed instructions about the administration of Judea (Josephus, *Ant.* 12.138–144). In this letter, the Seleucid king is said to have instructed: "All who belong to the people are to be governed in accordance with their ancestral laws [*politeuésthōsan dè pántes hoi ek toũ éthnous katà toùs patríous nómous*]"

---

[12] In a papyrus dated 226 BCE (*CPJ* 1, no. 19), two Judeans litigate their case before an apparently non-Judean court in Krokodilopolis-Arsinoe (in the Fayum) according to the "civic laws (*politikoì nomoi*)." Mélèze-Modrzejewski has argued that for the Judeans, this term *must* refer to the Torah, and that the Septuagint was created to make the "civic laws of the Judeans" accessible to non-Judean judges (Mélèze-Modrzejewski 1996; 2001). For a different view of the term "civic laws" here, see Tcherikover 1957: 33n85. A very fragmentary papyrus dated 218 BCE (*CPJ* 1, no. 128) has been reconstructed as referring to an agreement "[in accordance with the c]ivic [law] of the [Ju]deans [(*katà tòn nómon p)olitikòn tõn (Iou)daíōn*]," but see the alternative reconstructions in Victor Tcherikover's commentary in *CPJ*, ad loc.). See also LeFebvre 2006: 146–82; Altmann 2021.

(Josephus, *Ant.* 12:142). Although many scholars regard this letter as authentic (e.g., Bickerman 2007a; Grabbe 2008a: 324–26), and several assume that the "ancestral laws" here refer to the laws of the Torah specifically (e.g., Tcherikover 1957: 7, 1959: 83–84; Bickerman 2007a: 355), the text itself provides no details about the actual *content* of these laws. Judeans would have been in no way unique in having their own set of "ancestral laws," and, as Elias Bickerman has noted, it was quite common in the Hellenistic world at this time for a conqueror to confirm a conquered city's "ancestral laws" just as Antiochus is said to have done for the Judeans (Bickerman 2007a: 341; Kratz 2024: 60–72).

Also in the previous section (Section 2.2), I cited a separate document Josephus alleges was sent by Antiochus III to the governor of Lydia, in which the king ordered that two thousand Judean families transported from Babylonia to Phrygia are to be allowed to "use their own laws [*nómois autoùs khrḗsthai toĩs idíois*]" (Josephus *Ant.* 12:150). Again, even if we were to accept this text as authentic, we would still not know if the laws of the Torah are necessarily what is referenced here.

A third document quoted by Josephus, a "proclamation" (*prógramma*) said to have been issued by Antiochus III, does provide some details about the Judean laws associated with the Jerusalem temple:

> It is unlawful for any foreigner to enter the enclosure of the temple which is forbidden to the Judeans, except to those of them who are accustomed to enter after purifying themselves in accordance with the ancestral law [*katà tòn pátrion nómon*]. Nor shall anyone bring into the city the flesh of horses, or of mules, or of wild or tame asses, or of leopards, foxes, or hares, or, in general, of any animals forbidden to the Judeans. Nor is it lawful to bring in their skins or even to breed any of these animals in the city. But only the sacrificial animals known to their ancestors and necessary for the propitiation of the deity shall they be permitted to use. And the person who violates any of these statutes shall pay to the priests a fine of three thousand drachmas of silver (Josephus, *Ant.* 12:145–46).

While scholars often read the ordinances cited here through the lens of later interpretations of Torah law (e.g., Bickerman 2007b; Orian 2020; Rhyder 2024), such readings are by no means obvious or even necessary. The Pentateuch itself does *not* preclude the entrance of non-Israelites into the sanctuary enclosure, nor does it prohibit bringing the flesh or skins of forbidden animals into the city (or surrounding camp) where the sanctum is located. It does *not* forbid breeding any such animals in the city (or surrounding camp), nor does it forbid the use of nonsacrificial animals or species deemed unacceptable for sacrifices. And while it is true that the species listed here would have been prohibited as food according to the criteria for quadrupeds in

Lev 11:1–8 and Deut 14:3–8, the horse, mule, ass, leopard, and fox are hardly obvious choices to specify for one who had in mind these Pentateuchal rules. If not the Torah, then what might the author of this alleged "proclamation" have had in view when listing specifically these regulations? It would not be surprising if the Jerusalem temple had its own unique, traditional set of sacred ordinances regulating who and what was allowed into the central Judean sanctuary and its sacred city. Indeed, several scholars have pointed to parallels between the rules specified in this document and temple ordinances found elsewhere throughout the Hellenistic world (e.g., Bickerman 2007b; Rhyder 2024). None of this would necessitate a widely recognized Mosaic Torah that had already come to govern the cult in and around the Jerusalem temple (Kratz 2024: 67).

3.2.4 The Wisdom of Joshua Ben Sira

The work known as the Wisdom of Joshua Ben Sira frequently refers to the concept of divine instruction or law, "*tôrâ*" (Greek: "*nómos*"), and divine commandment, "*miṣwâ*" (Greek: "*entolḗ*") (see Schnabel 1985: 40–41). The original Hebrew version of the work is commonly dated sometime around the first quarter of the second century BCE, while its Greek translation – purportedly by the author's own grandson – is thought to have been completed toward the end of the same century (Williams 1994).

There has been some debate within scholarship over precisely what Ben Sira meant when he used these terms, as he provided very little details about the content of this "instruction," "law," or "commandment." Although some scholars assume these terms to mean Mosaic legislation as found in the Pentateuch, others have argued that the author intended a more universal kind of natural law (see Wright 2013: 157–59, n3–6).

Even if Pentateuchal law is meant, we must remember that Ben Sira was a highly educated intellectual, and accordingly was not representative of the broader Judean populace. The extent to which ordinary Judeans might have already been observing Torah law, if at all, is impossible to determine from the writings of Ben Sira on their own.

3.3 Conclusions

The data we have reviewed here provide no compelling evidence to suggest that Judeans at large, whether in Judea or abroad, regarded the Torah as authoritative or even knew of its existence any time during the Early Hellenistic period. This largely resembles the situation in the preceding Persian period, from which time we similarly lack any compelling evidence for widespread Torah observance or knowledge. In both periods – as in earlier times – Judeans would presumably have had customary civil and ritual regulations according to which they would have organized their communal, familial, and personal lives. It would not be until the rise of the Hasmoneans, however, that we begin to find evidence indicating that *the Torah* served as the foundation for the Judeans' operative legal system.

Cultic matters comprise a significant and sizable component of Pentateuchal legislation. Among its detailed regulations surrounding the priesthood and the sacrificial system that the priests were to follow, we find the insistence that YHWH is to be worshiped at a centralized sanctuary and to the exclusion of any other deities. If the Torah was not yet regarded as authoritative in the Early Hellenistic period, we might inquire as to the precise character of Judean cultic practices during this era. Specifically, it bears asking if and to what degree the Judean cult may have become centralized and exclusive at this time. It is to these questions that we now turn.

4 Cultic Worship of YHWH

As early as the middle of the ninth century BCE, the cultic worship of YHWH among Israelites finds mention in the Mesha Stele (lines 17–18; see Jackson and Dearman 1989: 94). YHWH as a deity revered by what were likely Israelites occurs frequently at the late ninth- or early eighth-century BCE site Kuntillet ʿAjrud (Aḥituv, Eshel, and Meshel 2012), and inscriptions mentioning hundreds of individuals with names bearing Yahwistic theophoric elements (*yhw-*, *yw-*, *-yhw*, *-yh*, and *-yw*) are known from dozens of late Iron Age sites in both Israel and Judea (Golub 2023). During the Persian period as well, widespread reverence for YHWH among Judeans is attested in Yahwistic elements included in the personal names of Judeans preserved in the epigraphic record from Judea and the diaspora, especially Elephantine and Babylonia (Zadok 1988). At Elephantine, this deity (known there as YHW or YHH) was worshiped in his own temple, his blessings were invoked in salutations included in correspondences, by his name various oaths were sworn, and on his behalf monies were collected (Granerød 2016). The entirety of the late Iron Age and Persian-era evidence suggests that by this time, YHWH had come to be revered as the primary Judean deity (even if other deities were also revered – see below).

During the Early Hellenistic period, personal names bearing Yahwistic theophoric elements continued to be popular among Judeans. In Judea, such names were either prefixed with "*yhw-*" or else suffixed with "*-yh*" (Ilan 2002), while in Egypt Yahwistic names were also sometimes prefixed with "*yw-*," or suffixed with "*-yhw*" or "*-yw*" (Ilan 2008).[13]

In the present section, we will examine what is known about how Judeans worshiped YHWH during the Early Hellenistic period. We will survey what is known about cultic sites dedicated to the worship of YHWH at Jerusalem, elsewhere in the Southern Levant, and in Egypt. Following this, we will explore the degree to which Early Hellenistic-period Judeans may have still revered, or at least acknowledged, other deities alongside YHWH.

4.1 Yahwistic Cultic Sites

4.1.1 The Temple in Jerusalem

Precious little information has survived from the Early Hellenistic period that informs us about the Jerusalem temple and the cultic activities which took place there. As noted in Section 2.1.2, a letter sent from the Judean community in Elephantine in 407 BCE refers to a petition which had been sent to "*yəhôḥānān*" the high priest and his colleagues, the priests who are in Jerusalem" (*TAD*, A4.7:18; see also A4.8:17), which suggests that at this time the high priest was situated at the apex of a hierarchy of priests, all of whom likely served as cultic officiants in a Jerusalem temple. There we also noted that a late-fourth-century BCE coin minted in Judea and which bears the legend "*yôḥānyâ* the priest" (*hakkôhēn*) (*YC*, type 25), likely refers to a high priest who served in what may have been a similar role at the start of the Early Hellenistic period (Figure 5). No other inscriptional or archaeological evidence relating directly to the Jerusalem temple, its cult or its priesthood, has survived from the Early Hellenistic period. Any surviving material remains of this temple are likely buried beneath the late-first-century BCE Temple Mount enclosure constructed by Herod the Great, and hence are currently inaccessible to archaeological examination.

Most of the literary sources which refer to the Jerusalem temple and its cult during the Ptolemaic and early Seleucid periods were written many years after the time they claim to portray (e.g., the alleged citation from Hecataeus of Abdera, discussed in Section 3.2.1, the Letter of Aristeas, and the writings of Flavius Josephus). Portrayals of the temple and its priestly cult in Ben Sira, probably from the first quarter of the second century BCE, provide mostly generic descriptions of a temple cult. In Sir 50:11–21, the author poetically

---

[13] This observation refers only to names recorded on papyri, ostraca, coins, and stone inscriptions, and which date to the Early Hellenistic period. Names preserved in literary sources are not considered here. I have also not considered here names from Aramaic ostraca found in Idumea, as these may belong to individuals who did not identify as Judeans (pace Zadok 2021: 234–35; see note 17 in this Element).

describes the officiation of the high priest, Simon son of Onias, upon an altar situated in the courtyard of the temple (Hebrew: *'ezrat mīqdāš*). Clothed in priestly attire, and standing by the multiple arrays of firewood on the altar, Simon is described as receiving sacrificial portions (*nətāḥîm*) from the hands of his priestly brethren, "the sons of Aaron." These sacrificial rites are said to take place "before all the assembly of Israel."[14] After the altar service is completed, the priests sound metal trumpets, and all the people bow to the ground to the sound of song and with prayer "before the merciful one." The high priest then descends from the altar, raises his hands, and blesses the people with "the blessing of YHWH," in response to which the assembled people bow down a second time.

While it seems likely that the priests of the Jerusalem temple would have followed a cultic system that, as in other cults, would have included both communal and private offerings (animal sacrifices, meal offerings, libations, and incense burning) along with other assorted rites conducted according to a specific cultic calendar, the precise details of this system remain essentially unknown. The Pentateuch prescribes a detailed scheme of sacrifices and other cultic rites to be followed in the desert Tabernacle and later in "the place YHWH will choose" (Deut 12:5, 11, 14, ff.), and this system was eventually adopted as Torah law. However, as we have seen in Section 3 with regard to Pentateuchal legislation as a whole, it is essentially unknown whether the cultic system outlined in the Pentateuch was regarded as authoritative already during the Early Hellenistic period, and whether it was put into practice by the Jerusalem priesthood any time prior to the Hasmonean ascent to power in the middle of the second century BCE.

4.1.2 Yahwistic Cultic Sites Elsewhere in the Southern Levant

The instruction that all cultic offerings be made exclusively in "the place that YHWH will choose" is repeated several times throughout Deuteronomy (12:5, 11, 14; 14:23–25; 15:20; 16:2, 6–7, 11; 17:8–10; 18:6; 26:2; 31:11). Although it appears that these prescriptions were meant to centralize the cult at a single temple in Jerusalem, there is some evidence for the existence of YHWH temples located outside of Jerusalem during the Early Hellenistic period. As we shall presently see, such temples would have been located outside the boundaries of Judea itself, and accordingly may well have been established by Yahwists who themselves did not identify as Judeans. Nevertheless, we should not discount the possibility that self-identifying Judeans may have sometimes visited these sacred sites to offer sacrifices or to perform other cultic rites.

---

[14] The Greek here (Sir 50:15) has the high priest libate wine from a cup at the foot of the altar.

Excavations conducted by Yitzhak Magen between 1983 and 2003 on the summit of Mount Gerizim uncovered the remains of a large compound identified as a sacred precinct (Magen 2007). Magen identified at the site two stratigraphic phases: an early phase, which he dated to the Persian and Early Hellenistic periods (mid fifth century to early second century BCE), and a late phase, dated from the time of Antiochus III to around 110 BCE when the site was destroyed by John Hyrcanus I (Magen 2007: 158–60).[15] Several hundred inscriptions in Aramaic, Hebrew and Greek on stones memorialize the names of worshipers and priests who offered sacrifices at the site (Magen, Misgav and Tsfania 2004). The excavators dated most of these inscriptions, on paleographic grounds, to the third and second centuries BCE, but noted that "some may belong to the earliest period of the sacred precinct (fifth–fourth centuries BCE)" (Magen, Misgav, and Tsfania 2004: 14). The fact that many of the personal names contain Yahwistic theophoric elements, that one Hebrew inscription mentions YHWH (Magen, Misgav, and Tsfania 2004: 254 [no. 383]), that another Hebrew inscription on a silver ring reads "*YHWH 'eḥād*" ("the one YHWH") (Magen, Misgav, and Tsfania 2004: 260–61 [no. 391]), and that a Greek inscription reads "to the God Most High" (*Theõi Hupsístōi*) (Magen 2008: 156) all point to YHWH as the divinity worshiped at this sanctuary. As the site is located deep within the territory of Samaria, it seems likely that the temple's priests and worshipers would have come primarily from the region and therefore probably would not have identified as Judeans. Nevertheless, we should not discount the possibility that Judean pilgrims might have also been attracted to a YHWH temple in neighboring Samaria (Barnea 2024: 12). Indeed, Gad Barnea has suggested that a fragmentary inscription which preserves the word "*[y]hwd*" (Magen, Misgav, and Tsfania 2004: 81 [no. 43]) may represent just such a person from Judea (*yəhûd*) who brought an offering at Gerizim.[16]

Among the corpus of Aramaic ostraca acquired on the antiquity market is one which mentions a YHWH shrine, which may have been functioning in Idumea during the late Persian or Early Hellenistic period (Yardeni 2016: 114). Although unprovenanced, the ostraca in this corpus are thought to derive from Khirbet el-Kom (ca. thirteen kilometers west of Hebron) and are dated

---

[15] The initial phase of construction has been called into question by other scholars, with some arguing for an earlier date, in the late Iron Age (Arie 2021), and others arguing for a later date, closer to the time of the Macedonian conquest in the late fourth century BCE (Mor 2011). This later dating aligns well with the account of Josephus (*Ant.* 11:321), according to which Sanaballétēs, the satrap of Samaria at the time of Alexander the Great, built a temple at Mt. Gerizim and installed as its high priest his own son-in-law (who also happened to have been the brother of the current Judean high priest in Jerusalem).

[16] Personal communication, May 30, 2024. I thank Gad for kindly allowing me to mention his hypothesis here. Note that Barnea (2024) has argued for the idea that during the Persian period, all believers in YHWH were identified as "*yəhûdîm/yəhûdāyē'*," and not just to those from Judea.

to the fourth century BCE. In describing a parcel of land, the ostracon mentions a "*ḥyb°l' zî bêt YHW*," which has been interpreted variously as "the ruin/precinct/region of the house of YHW" (Yardeni 2016: 114; Zadok 2021: 180). If "precinct" or "region" is accepted rather than "ruin," it would suggest the existence of a functioning Yahwistic temple or shrine during the fourth century BCE, perhaps at Khirbet el-Kom itself (Becking 2008). Although such a temple would most likely have been used by local Idumeans, as at Gerizim we should not discount the prospect of Judeans visiting and offering sacrifices at the site.[17]

At Lachish, located in what was likely Idumean territory, excavations unearthed a cultic structure containing an altar which, although originally dated to the Persian period, was later dated by Yohanan Aharoni to the Hellenistic period (Aharoni 1968; 1975; see also Tal 2006: 69). Because of the similarity of its plan to the Iron Age temple in Arad, Aharoni suggested that the structure was built by Judeans as a "traditional Israelite shrine" dedicated to the worship of YHWH (Aharoni 1968: 161–64, 1975: 11).[18] Considering that the Lachish shrine was built several centuries after the Arad temple was destroyed, however, the ostensible resemblance of the two structures fails to provide sufficient grounds to extrapolate that this was a YHWH shrine or that it was used by Judeans.[19]

4.1.3 Yahwistic Cultic Sites in Egypt

As noted on several occasions previously, a Judean temple at Elephantine dedicated to the cult of YHWH (locally known as YHW) was in existence until its destruction in 410 BCE. While we know that the local community sought to rebuild this temple soon after it had been razed, it is unclear if they succeeded in their efforts. The last documents from the Judeans of Elephantine date to around 399 BCE, and it remains unknown what happened to the community after this time. The fact that a Judean YHWH temple existed at Elephantine until as late as 410 BCE raises the question if similar temples might have existed elsewhere in Egypt in the subsequent centuries.

---

[17] Within the entire corpus of unprovenanced Aramaic ostraca thought to be from Idumea are twenty-one names bearing a Yahwistic theophoric element (Zadok 2021: 207, 209). While Ran Zadok assumes that these are likely to have belonged to Judeans (Zadok 2021: 234–35), I see it no less likely that these names might have belonged to local Idumean Yahwists.

[18] In support of his suggestion for an active YHWH cult at Lachish in the centuries following the Iron Age, Aharoni noted that a Hebrew or Aramaic inscription on a small incense altar dated to the Persian period includes either a dedication to YHWH or else a name with a Yahwistic theophoric element (Aharoni 1968: 163–64, 1975: 5–7). Others, however, have offered readings of this inscription which have nothing to do with the tetragrammaton; see, for example, Lemaire 2015: 99.

[19] Similarly unconvincing is the suggestion that a Hellenistic-era temple at Beersheba resembling those at Arad and Lachish was a Judean temple of YHWH (contra Derfler 1993). The Qaṣr el-ʿAbd compound at ʿIrāq al-Amīr has also been identified by some as a Hellenistic-era Judean temple, but this too is unlikely (see Will 1983).

Sylvie Honigman has argued that in fact a Judean YHWH temple like the one at Elephantine likely existed in Edfu during the Early Hellenistic period, as a third century BCE Aramaic papyrus from this community (*TAD*, C3.28 [=*CPJ* 4, no. 525]) mentions two or three Judean priests (Honigman 2009: 121–23). According to Honigman, the term "priest" (*kāhănā'*) appended to the personal names of these individuals appears to represent their occupation – rather than simply an abstract title signifying priestly lineage – and therefore we may presume that they conducted ritual service in a temple. Building on this hypothesis, Barnea has speculated that the Judean community of Edfu may have originated from a migration of the Elephantine community itself after it became clear that their temple would not be rebuilt (Barnea 2021: 182–83).

While the notion of a third-century BCE YHWH temple at Edfu remains somewhat speculative, dedicatory inscriptions on limestone plaques from this same period testify to the existence of a Judean institution called a "(place of) prayer" (*proseukhḗ*). The two earliest of these inscriptions (*JIGRE*, nos. 22 and 117) state that the dedication was accomplished "on behalf of" (*hupèr*) a King Ptolemy and Queen Berenice, commonly identified as Ptolemy III Euergetes and Berenice II Euergetis, coregents from 246 to 221 BCE (Figure 8).[20] Very

Figure 8 Stone plaque from Schedia (near Alexandria, Egypt) with Greek inscription dedicating a Judean "(place of) prayer" (*proseukhḗ*) (*JIGRE*, no. 22); 246–221 BCE (Drawing: Yuliya Shmidov; after *JIGRE*, plate IX).

---

[20] One inscription was discovered in Schedia (southeast of Alexandria), while the second inscription was purchased from an antiquities dealer in Medinet el-Fayum near the site of ancient Krokodilopolis-Arsinoe (the inscription itself mentions "the Ju[dean]s in Krok[o]dilopolis").

similar inscriptions, with the identical loyalty formula of dedication "on behalf of" the king or royal family, were common in contemporary temples in both Egypt and other Hellenistic kingdoms (Fraser 1972: 116). Other, somewhat later Ptolemaic-era inscriptions suggest that Judean "(places of) prayer" were located in purpose-built structures, which at least sometimes had a "gateway" (*pulṓn*) and an adjacent "exedra" (*JIGRE*, nos. 24 and 28). One inscription of unknown origin purports to replace an earlier plaque upon which a "King Ptolemy Euergetes" (i.e., either Ptolemy III, who reigned 246–221 BCE, or Ptolemy VIII, who reigned 145–116 BCE) is said to have granted to the *proseukhḗ* the right of asylum (*ásulon*) – a privilege usually granted to temples (*JIGRE*, nos. 125).[21] And finally, a papyrus dated on paleographic grounds to the third century BCE mentions contributions to a "*proseu[khḗ]*" by a list of named individuals presumed to be Judeans (*CPJ* 4, no. 619). Unfortunately, these and other such inscriptions provide precious little information to help otherwise understand the form or function of this institution, and no buildings associated with any of these inscriptions have been identified to date. While the name of the institution suggests that its central purpose was to serve as a communal site for offering prayers, we should probably not discount the possibility that *proseukhḗ* compounds may have also served as sites for the performance of other cultic activities, like burning incense and offering vegetable and animal sacrifices. Indeed, Anders Runesson has argued that the Early Hellenistic *proseukhaí* in Egypt were for all intents and purposes Judean temples dedicated to the cult of YHWH (Runesson 2001: 429–36).

4.2 Reverence for Other Deities alongside YHWH

"I am YHWH your God, who brought you out of the land of Egypt, out of the house of slavery; you shall have no other gods before me" (Exod 20:2; Deut 5:6). While insistence upon worship of YHWH alone, to the exclusion of any and all other deities, features as a leitmotif throughout much of the Hebrew Bible, these same texts repeatedly pose accusations about the Israelite and Judean masses commonly venerating other gods and goddesses alongside YHWH. That Judeans did in fact continue to revere other deities as late as the second half of the fifth century BCE becomes evident in the documents from Elephantine, which depict a Judean community that worshiped YHWH as their primary deity while concomitantly venerating multiple deities other than

---

[21] A Ptolemaic-era papyrus (*CPJ* 1, no. 129) which mentions a man escaping into a Judean *proseukhḗ* may provide an example of just such a right of asylum in action; see Tcherikover's commentary in *CPJ* 1, 240–41. The document also mentions a caretaker of the *proseukhḗ* called a "*neōkóros*," a title known from neighboring pagan cults as a member of a temple's personnel; see Tcherikover's commentary there.

YHWH (Granerød 2016; Barnea 2021). Cuneiform documents from around the same time in Babylonia suggest a similar picture for Judean communities in the Mesopotamian diaspora (Alstola 2020: 141, 161–63, 213–18, 267–72). In what follows, we will explore the evidence from the subsequent Early Hellenistic period to try and determine whether and to what extent Judeans may have continued to revere gods other than YHWH during the century and a half following the conquests of Alexander the Great.

4.2.1 Athena Motifs on Judean Coins

Coins minted by the Judean authorities in Jerusalem during the late Persian period and into the Early Hellenistic period include motifs clearly linked to Athena. From the Persian period are at least six coin types (*YC*, types 3–8) that display on the obverse the helmeted head of Athena and on the reverse the owl famously associated with the Greek goddess.[22] As these coin types are visibly imitations of already widely circulating Athenian prototypes, however, many scholars have downplayed the significance of these images as having lost any "religious" meaning among those who minted and used the coins (Meshorer 2001: 7; Gitler, Lorber, and Fontanille 2023: 161).

Five coin types dated to the first three decades following the conquests of Alexander the Great (*YC*, types 24–28) display on the obverse a facing head framed by a dotted border and on the reverse the owl of Athena. Haim Gitler, Catharine Lorber, and Jean-Philippe Fontanille (2023: 178) have provided the most recent and compelling interpretation of the image on the obverse, explaining that it depicts an oval shield ornamented with a gorgoneion. According to these scholars, the pairing of the shield with the gorgoneion device on the obverse and the owl on the reverse suggests that the gorgoneion represents the aegis of Athena and symbolizes her protective power as a war goddess. These scholars rightly note that, unlike the Persian-era coins, which simply imitate prototypes from Athens, these Early Hellenistic coins represent a novel composition of Athena motifs completely unique to these Judean coins (Gitler, Lorber, and Fontanille 2023: 178–79). With this in mind, it is quite remarkable that on the reverses of two of these types, directly next to the owl of Athena, appear the names and titles of two Judean authorities: "*yəḥizqiyyâ* the governor" (*happeḥâ*) (on *YC*, type 24) (Figure 4) and "*yôḥānyâ* the priest" (*hakkôhēn*) (on *YC*, type 25) (Figure 5). Not only are both names Yahwistic, the latter almost certainly held the office of high priest in the Jerusalem temple of YHWH. How

---

[22] On three additional types dated to the Persian period and with an owl on the reverse (*YC*, types 9–11), the figure on the obverse has been interpreted variously as Athena or as a male, either the Persian king or a local authority (see Gitler, Lorber and Fontanille 2023: 162–65).

Between Yahwism and Judaism   43

are we to reconcile the employment of motifs associated with a deity other than YHWH by Judean authorities, one of whom was the high priest of Jerusalem?

A simplistic answer would be to assume that any association with Athena symbolism was either unknown to the Judean minting authorities, or else ignored by them as unimportant. There are good reasons, however, to consider the very real possibility that use of these images was not an oversight, but rather reflects a common Judean acknowledgement – if not outright veneration – of the warrior goddess. The Greek Athena was identified among easterners with the West Semitic goddess Anat (Louden 2006: 240–85; Bianco and Bonnet 2016). At Elephantine, one undated document tells of an oath taken by one Judean to another in the name of "Ḥ[erem?] the [god] in/by the place of prostration [bəmisgādā'] and by Anathyahu [ûva'ănātYHW]" (*TAD*, B7.3:3). While the precise meaning of the name Anathyahu is not at all self-evident, a plausible interpretation is that it means "Anat of YHW" and refers to the Semitic goddess Anat as the female consort of YHW (Granerød 2016: 250–52). Another document, usually dated to either 419 or 400 BCE, contains a lengthy accounting of the names of individual members of "the garrison of the Judeans" who "gave silver to YHW the god [zî yəhav kəsaf ləYHW 'ĕlāhā']," after which it is noted that the entire sum was divided among three deities: YHW, Eshembethel, and Anathbethel (*TAD*, C3.15). Again, while the meaning of Anathbethel is not obvious, a likely explanation is that it refers to Anat as the female consort of the deity Bethel (Granerød 2016: 256). These documents clearly demonstrate that toward the end of the fifth century BCE, Yahwist Judeans at Elephantine regarded Anat as a deity by whom one might swear an oath and to whom one might donate silver. Is it at all farfetched, then, to interpret the images of Athena on the mid to late fourth-century BCE coins minted in Jerusalem as a reflection of Judean Yahwists' view of Anat/Athena as a deity to be recognized, if not revered, alongside the primary cult of YHWH?[23] If this interpretation is correct, it is significant that these were circulating coins minted by both a Judean governor and a Judean high priest, which suggests that the phenomenon was less than fringe.

4.2.2 Inscriptions in Temples of Greek Deities

An inscription unearthed at Oropos (in East Attica, Greece) in the Amphiareion, a sanctuary dedicated to the cultic worship of the divine hero Amphiaraus,

---

[23] Compare with a coin type minted around this time in Samaria which displays the Yahwistic name "*yəhô'ānâ*" (in Aramaic script) on the obverse and "Zeus" (in Greek) on the reverse (*SC*, no. 40). For Athena on a bulla from a building excavated in the Givʿati Parking Lot in Jerusalem, see Shalom et al. 2021. If this bulla was attached to a document sent from abroad, however, it might not be representative of specifically Judean beliefs and practices.

Figure 9 Stone stele from Oropos (in East Attica, Greece) with Greek inscription describing how a Judean named Moschus son of Moschion paid homage to the Greek deities Amphiaraus and Hygeia (*IJO* 1, Ach45); first half of the third century BCE (Photo: Mitsos 1952: 195).

presents what is perhaps the most direct indication of a person self-identifying as a "Judean" who paid homage to deities other than YHWH (Figure 9). Dated on paleographic grounds to the first half of the third century BCE, the inscription is a manumission stele which declares the freedom of a certain Judean named Moschus, son of Moschion. Following a statement on the terms of the manumission and the names of five witnesses to the act, the inscription proceeds to inform its readers that Moschus erected the stele himself following a divine vision: "Moschus (son) of Moschion, a Judean (*Ioudaĩos*), (set this up), having seen a dream with the god Amphiaraus and Hygeia commanding (him), in accordance with what Amphiaraus and Hygeia ordered, to write it on a stele and set it up by the altar" (*IJO* 1, Ach45:11–15). Immediately after self-identifying as a Judean, Moschus proceeds without pause to describe his obedience to the instructions of "the god" Amphiaraus and the goddess Hygeia, as he claims to have received in a dream, in writing the stele and setting it up by the altar of the Amphiareion. The editors of *IJO* have suggested that perhaps Moschus regarded Amphiaraus and

Hygeia "as angelic or magical powers rather than deities" (Noy, Panayotov, and Bloedhorn 2004: 179), but this seems to be little more than a case of special pleading.

Two votive inscriptions presented by individuals directly identifying as "Judeans," along with another two inscriptions by individuals with names thought to be Judean, were found at the temple of Pan at El-Kanais (in the desert east of Edfu, Egypt) (*JIGRE*, nos. 121–24). Here, too, apologetic explanations have been offered to explain the presence of Judeans in a temple to a Greek deity (see Horbury and Noy 1992: 207–9), but these remain unconvincing. All four inscriptions were hesitantly dated, on the basis of paleography, to the second or first centuries BCE. If this dating is correct, it would suggest that at least some Judeans may have continued to venerate deities other than YHWH well into the Hellenistic period.

4.2.3 Letter Sent by Toubias

A letter sent by a certain Toubias, who appears to have been a Judean aristocrat living east of the Jordan, to a Ptolemaic official in Egypt and dated 257 BCE, opens with the following greeting: "If you and all your affairs are flourishing, and everything else is as you wish it, many thanks to the gods (*pollḕ kháris toîs theoîs*)!" (*CPJ* 1, no. 4) (Figure 10). While the reference to a plurality of "gods" here is striking, the fact that Toubias held a unique socio-economic position prevents us from assuming that such an attitude might have been especially prevalent within Judean society at large.

4.2.4 The Judean Onomasticon

Judeans with personal names bearing theophoric elements associated with deities other than YHWH are well documented within the Early Hellenistic epigraphic record. A search for such names within the Judean onomasticon in the western diaspora collected by Tal Ilan (2008) produces the following names from the third century BCE – all from Egypt: Apollodorus and Apollonius (referring to the Greek god Apollo); Artemidorus (referring to the Greek goddess Artemis); Aphroditus (referring to the Greek goddess Aphrodite); Demetrius (referring to the Greek goddess Demeter); Diodotus, Diocles, and Diophantus (referring to the Greek god Zeus); Dionysius (referring to the Greek god Dionysus); Eutychas (referring to the Greek goddess Tyche); Hermias (referring to the Greek god Hermes); Heracleia and Heracleides (referring to the Greek divine hero Heracles); Isidorus (referring to the Egyptian goddess Isis); and Zenodora and Zenon (referring, again, to Zeus). A similar search within the Judean onomasticon in the Southern Levant also collected by

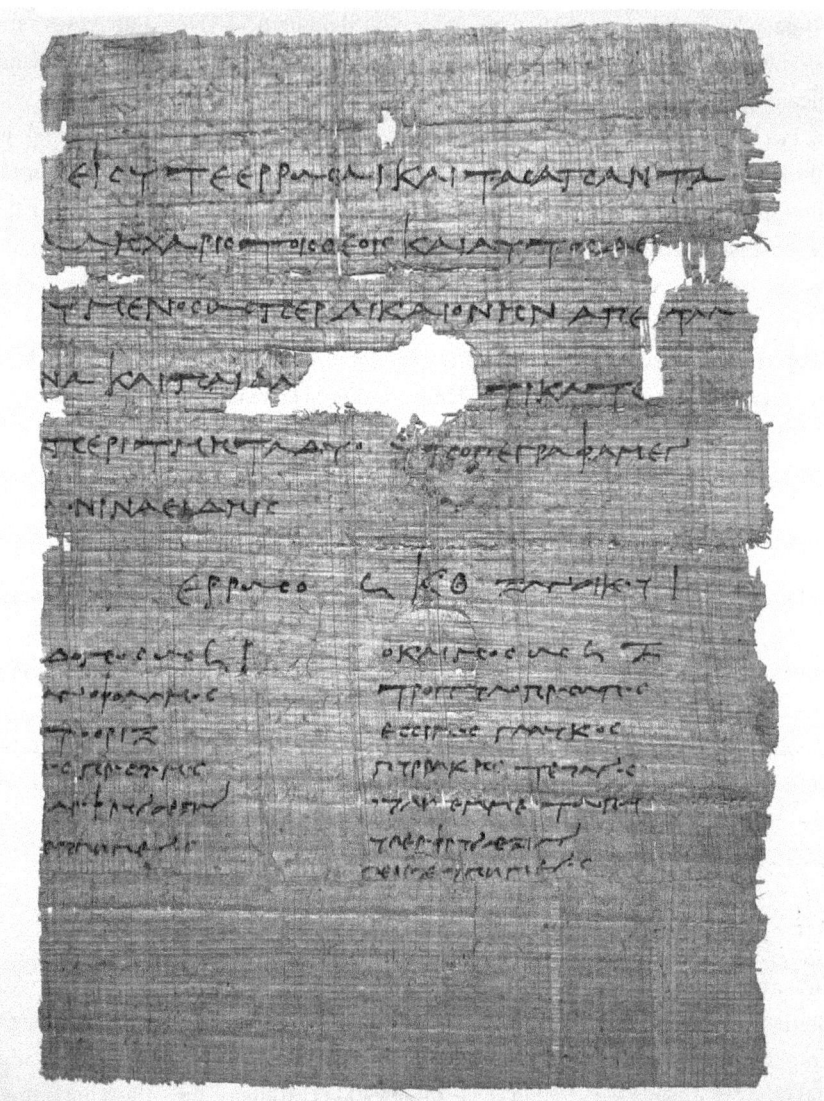

Figure 10 Fragment of papyrus letter sent by Toubias to a Ptolemaic official, opening with the Greek formula "many thanks to the gods" (*CPJ* 1, no. 4); 257 BCE (Photo: From the British Library Collection: Papyrus 2684).

Ilan (2002) produces no such names from the Early Hellenistic period (although many names of this sort do appear there in later periods; see Ilan 2002: 10–11).[24]

---

[24] This observation refers only to names recorded on papyri, ostraca, coins, and stone inscriptions; names preserved in literary sources are not considered here.

While these observations may be suggestive of a certain willingness among Judean parents in Egypt, but not in Judea, to memorialize non-Yahwistic deities in the names of their children, some qualifications are in order. On the one hand, several of the names listed above belong to individuals whose identification as Judeans is uncertain. On the other hand, it seems quite likely that the epigraphic record includes an untold number of Judeans with names bearing theophoric elements of deities other than YHWH, but who have never been identified as Judeans because indications of their Judean identity have not survived. Considering these caveats, we should exercise caution before attempting to reach conclusions about the prevalence of such naming patterns in either Judea or the diaspora.

Even if we were to assume that our list of names was largely representative, we ought exercise caution in interpreting this data. Although it does seem quite possible that all these names continued to maintain their divine associations, it is hard to be sure of this. Many Judeans may have simply shared in the naming trends of the larger cultural milieus within which they were embedded without paying too much attention to the original "religious" meanings of the names (Tcherikover 1957: 29).

4.2.5 The Ptolemaic Royal Family in Egyptian Proseukhḗ Inscriptions

Above, we saw in that in two inscriptions from Egypt dated to the second half of the third century BCE, the local Judean community dedicated a "(place of) prayer" (*proseukhḗ*) in honor of the Ptolemaic king and queen (*JIGRE*, nos. 22 and 117) (Figure 8). More precisely, the dedications were said to have been made "on behalf of" (*hupèr*) the royal couple, which, as we have seen, was a formula of loyalty common in dedicatory inscriptions from contemporary temples (Fraser 1972: 116). Unlike temple inscriptions, however, the Judean *proseukhḗ* inscriptions omit the term "god (*theós*)" when describing the Ptolemaic monarchs. It seems likely that this was a deliberate omission, meant to avoid ascribing divinity to the royal figures (Fraser 1972: 282–83). Accordingly, it may suggest a more general avoidance of recognizing deities other than YHWH among members of the Judean communities represented by these inscriptions, at least within the context of the *proseukhḗ* itself.

4.3 Conclusions

As in the preceding Iron Age and Persian era, Judeans continued to worship YHWH as their primary deity throughout the Early Hellenistic period. Although the Jerusalem temple probably served as a preeminent site for the Yahwistic cult, very little is known about the nature of the cultic system in place there. To the extent that at this time Judeans may have also conducted Yahwistic cultic activities *outside of* Jerusalem, and to the degree that Judeans may have venerated *other deities alongside* YHWH, the Early Hellenistic period would mark an era of significant continuity with the historic eras that preceded it. While there are certain tantalizing indications that the noncentralized, nonexclusive Yahwism of the Iron Age and Persian era continued to characterize Judean cult well into the Early Hellenistic period, it remains difficult to sketch its contours or its prevalence in any significant detail. Whatever the precise character of Early Hellenistic Judean cult, none of this appears to resemble what we find in the subsequent Hasmonean and Early Roman periods, when Judean worship came to be centered exclusively on a single deity, and the Jerusalem temple developed into the sole legitimate site for sacrificial worship and pilgrimage.

Until now, our investigation has focused entirely on internal matters relating to Judeans' administrative, legal and cultic systems. We have seen that all of these display a noteworthy degree of continuity with the preceding Persian period, with little evidence of significant disruption. That said, we have yet to engage with the proverbial "elephant in the room." The Macedonian armies undoubtably brought with them an entire suite of Greek cultural elements which were largely new to the East. These would eventually come to exert profound influence on Judean culture. In the following section, we will ask whether this influence comes into view already in the Early Hellenistic period.

5 Adoption of Greek Cultural Elements

A copious amount of scholarship has been dedicated to the encounter of Judeans with Greek culture in the centuries that followed the conquests of Alexander the Great. Earlier scholarship assumed that "Hellenism" (a modern concept variously defined) was fundamentally antithetical to "Judaism" (another largely modern term). Using this confrontational paradigm as a lens, scholars investigated the degree to which Judeans either "assimilated" or else "resisted" Greek influences. More recent treatments have recognized that Hellenism and Judaism were not mutually exclusive, and have instead shifted to interrogate the various ways that Judeans absorbed and adapted Greek cultural traits into what scholars have come to call "Hellenistic Judaism" (for a history of this scholarship, see Grabbe 2008a: 126–36).

To properly investigate the encounter of Judeans with Hellenism would require us to characterize the phenomenon more broadly in terms of the encounter of Greek culture with the many and sundry other identity groups which came under Greek sway following the Macedonian incursion into the

East. As the scope of our study does not allow for this, the present section will instead be far more narrowly focused. It will examine primary evidence relating to Judean contact with three cultural elements which the ancients would have likely associated specifically with "Greekness": Greek language, Greek names, and Greek-styled material culture. It will ask not only if and where Judeans may have taken on these cultural elements, but also whether their adoption would have signaled a substantial break with earlier Judean culture.

5.1 Greek Language

5.1.1 Judea

Although some earlier studies have argued that the Greek language made significant inroads in Judea as early as the third century BCE (Hengel 1974: 1.58–65; Barr 1989: 102), the current state of the evidence does not appear to bear this assessment. To the contrary, the albeit patchy numismatic and epigraphic record from Early Hellenistic Judea suggests the continued use of Aramaic and Hebrew, with hardly any employment of Greek.

Twenty-seven coin types are identified as having been minted in Judea during the early years of Macedonian rule and under the first Ptolemaic kings (*YC*, types 18–44). On almost all these types, the legend (either the personal name and title of the minting authority or the name of the province) is written exclusively in Hebrew, in Paleo-Hebrew script (*YC*, types 18–19, 24–26, 30–37, 39, 41, 43–44). The few exceptions include one apparently pre-Ptolemaic type displaying a blundered Greek legend that appears to include fragments from the word "*basiléōs*" ("of the king") and "*hiereús*" ("priest") (*YC*, type 27). Another pre-Ptolemaic type displays various unintelligible pseudo-Greek inscriptions (*YC*, type 28). The blundered Greek on these two early types suggests that the Judean die engravers who designed them were essentially illiterate in Greek (Fontanille and Lorber 2008: 48). On only one exceptionally rare Ptolemaic type (only two examples are known), a clear Greek inscription featuring the letters "BA" – probably an abbreviation of the Greek royal title "*basileús*" ("king") – appears directly adjacent to the Paleo-Hebrew legend "*yəhūdâ*" ("Judea") (*YC*, type 42) (Figure 11). This is among the latest of the Judean coins with Paleo-Hebrew legends, thought to have been minted around the middle of the third century BCE, perhaps even as late as 242/1 BCE; after this, the Judean mint went out of service (Gitler, Lorber and Fontanille 2023: 121–24). The continued minting of coins with Hebrew legends until almost a century after the conquests of Alexander the Great suggests that by this time Greek had yet to make any significant inroads among the general populace of Judea.

Figure 11 Silver coin from Judea; obverse: image of Ptolemy II Philadelphus; reverse: eagle with Paleo-Hebrew legend "*yəhūdâ*" ("Judea") and the Greek letters "BA" ("*basileús*"; "king") (*YC*, type 42); after 261/0 BCE (Photo: from the collection of Dr. David and Jemima Jeselsohn, Zurich, Switzerland).

Similar conclusions may be drawn from the hundreds of stamp impressions found on Judean storage jar handles during this time (see above, Section 2.1.1), all of which are in Aramaic or Hebrew. Stamping jar handles appears to have been a well-established bureaucratic means to control the local system of collecting, distributing, and taxing oil and wine produced in Judea (Lipschits and Vanderhooft 2011). During the fourth and third centuries BCE, the stamps displayed the name of the province "*yəhūd*" in Paleo-Hebrew or Aramaic script, either as the three letters "*y-h-d*" or else in abbreviated form as "*y-h*" (Lipschits and Vanderhooft 2011: 253–592). Greek legends never appear on any of these administrative stamps, suggesting a lack of Greek proficiency among Judeans involved in this aspect of the local bureaucracy.

Relatively few ostraca unearthed in Judea proper have been dated to the Early Hellenistic period, but those which have are written in either Aramaic or Hebrew (e.g., Rosenbaum and Seger 1986; *CIIP*, nos. 613–15, 625, 629–30), even if these can sometimes include Greek loanwords (Cross 1981) (Figure 12).[25] A papyrus from a cave near Jericho (Jericho papList of Loans ar [Jer 1]) with a list of Judean names and tentatively assigned a late-fourth-century BCE date is similarly written in Aramaic (Eshel and Misgav 2000). To date, no Greek inscriptions dating to the Early Hellenistic period have a clear provenance in Judea.[26]

---

[25] I have excluded from the discussion here the large corpus of ostraca discovered in (or thought to derive from) Idumea – some of which date to the beginning of the Early Hellenistic period.

[26] A survey of the two volumes of the *CIIP* which cover Judea (Cotton et al. 2010–12; Ameling 2018) reveals only one Greek inscription dated to the Early Hellenistic period (*CIIP*, no. 1). The inscription, dated on the basis of its letter forms to either the third or second century BCE, was "said to have been found in a cart carrying rubble fill from the basement of an unidentified Arabic

Figure 12 Ostracon from Jerusalem (ca. fifty meters south of the western Hulda gate of the Temple Mount) in Aramaic but with Greek loanwords (*CIIP*, no. 615); late fourth or early third century BCE (Photo: courtesy of the IAA, by Miki Koren).

It seems likely that members of the Judean elite who were heavily invested in the bureaucracy of the Hellenistic kingdoms ruling Judea would have had to have learned at least some Greek in order to facilitate communication. Such a phenomenon may be reflected in two Greek papyri dated 257 BCE and sent to Ptolemaic authorities in Egypt by a certain Toubias, who appears to have been a Judean aristocrat living east of the Jordan, just outside of Judea proper (*CPJ* 1, nos. 4–5). Of course, we do not know to what degree such elite Judeans might have gained proficiency in speaking, reading, and writing Greek themselves, and to what extent they may have relied on personal translators and secretaries.

5.1.2 Egypt

Aramaic was the primary language used by Judeans living in Egypt during the Persian period, as is evidenced by the large assemblage of papyri and ostraca from Elephantine and elsewhere. Greek eventually replaced Aramaic as the written and spoken language of Egypt's Judeans, but it remains to be seen when and how quickly this linguistic shift occurred. Whereas earlier studies assumed a rather rapid rejection of Aramaic in favor of Greek beginning as early as the third century BCE (e.g., Hengel 1974: 1.58–65; Barr 1989: 102), the data provided by the epigraphic record available today paint a more complex picture.

---

house in the old city of Jerusalem," but the editors note: "it must be stressed that the provenance is very doubtful; the inscription may not be from Jerusalem at all."

Several Aramaic texts from Egypt which include the names of Judeans have been assigned dates in the Early Hellenistic period (third century or sometimes even early second century BCE), usually on the basis of paleography and/or the additional presence of Greek names (written in Aramaic script). These include sixteen ostraca, four of which were uncovered in excavations at Edfu (*TAD*, D8.6 [=*CPJ* 4, no. 533]; D8.13 [=*CPJ* 4, no. 522]; D9.15 [=*CPJ* 4, no. 539]; D11.26 [=*CPJ* 4, no. 540]) and the remainder of which were acquired on the antiquities market but are also thought to have derived from Edfu (*TAD*, D7.55–57 [=*CPJ* 4, nos. 527–529]; D8.3–5 [=*CPJ* 4, nos. 530–532]; D8.7–11 [=*CPJ* 4, nos. 534–538]; *CPJ* 4, no. 523). Two of these ostraca include exact dates, corresponding to 253 BCE (*CPJ* 4, no. 523) and 252 BCE (*TAD*, D8.13 [=*CPJ* 4, no. 522]). Three Aramaic epitaphs with Judean names unearthed in the El-Ibrahimiya necropolis of Alexandria have been dated to the "early Ptolemaic" period on the basis of paleography, as well as archaeological remains from elsewhere in the cemetery (*JIGRE*, nos. 3–5 [=*TAD*, D.21.4–6]). Nine Aramaic epitaphs containing Judean names from the old cemetery at Edfu have been dated paleographically to the late third or early second centuries BCE (*TAD*, D21.7–15 [=*CPJ* 4, "*JIGRE*," nos. 157–65]), as has one from Hagir Esna (Latopolis) (*TAD*, D21.16 [=*CPJ* 4, "*JIGRE*," no. 166]). Two Aramaic papyri containing the names of Judeans are thought to derive from Edfu, and have been dated paleographically to the third century BCE (*TAD*, C3.28 [=*CPJ* 4, no. 525]; D1.17 [=*CPJ* 4, no. 526]). Whether or not any of these documents or inscriptions were written by Judeans themselves (as seems likely), at the very least they suggest that various communities of Judeans in Egypt continued to live in Aramaic milieus well into the third century BCE, and perhaps even later.[27]

A significant number of Greek epigraphic and papyrological finds from Early Hellenistic Egypt mention Judeans and/or include names that have been identified as uniquely Judean. These include seven ostraca (*CPJ* 1, nos. 96–97; 112–13; 119; *CPJ* 4, nos. 524; 553), unprovenanced but mostly thought to derive from Upper Egypt. Three Greek epitaphs unearthed in the El-Ibrahimiya necropolis of Alexandria near the clearly Judean ones mentioned above contain names that may be Judean (*JIGRE*, nos. 6–8). Another Greek epitaph unearthed in the Hadra necropolis of Alexandria also displays a name that may be Judean (*JIGRE* no. 10). As discussed in Section 4.1.3, the Greek inscriptions on stone with the clearest association to Judeans are two dedicatory inscriptions which refer to a Judean "(place of) prayer" (*proseukhḗ*); one is from Schedia and the other is from Krokodilopolis-Arsinoe, and both are dated 246–221

---

[27] For the hypothesis that non-Judeans ceased to use Aramaic after the departure of the Persians, see Hacham and Ilan 2020: 27–28. For a single papyrus in Aramaic with no apparently Judean names, see *TAD*, C3.29 (=*CPJ* 4, no. 552).

BCE (*JIGRE*, nos. 22; 117). The largest group of Early Hellenistic-period Greek texts which refer to Judeans and/or that contain Judean names consists of seventy-two papyri from various sites throughout Egypt (*CPJ* 1, nos. 1–23; 33–40; 125–31; *CPJ* 4, nos. 554; 578; 585–95; 597–602; 607; 619). While only a small number of these texts are likely to have been written by Judeans themselves, the sum of this evidence suggests that by the third century BCE, several Judean communities in Egypt were already interacting directly, to one degree or another, with a Greek-speaking environment.

It is no simple task to interpret these epigraphic and papyrological data to draw general conclusions about the spread of Greek among Judean communities in Early Hellenistic Egypt. Whereas Aramaic is represented somewhat more frequently on the ostraca and stone inscriptions associated with Judeans, Greek dominates as the primary language used in the papyri. This may suggest, as Victor Tcherikover has argued, that Aramaic remained the *spoken language* of Judeans at the same time that Greek supplanted Aramaic as the *language of commerce* used in drawing up transactional documents (Tcherikover 1957: 30). It seems reasonable to conjecture that Greek proficiency would have been more important for the Judean elites involved with the Ptolemaic administration and with commercial interactions outside of the Judean community, and less for the remainder of the Judean masses who could probably continue to get by without learning much Greek. Another important variable is the findspots of the different inscriptions; whereas most of the Aramaic texts were (or appear to have been) unearthed in Edfu, the Greek texts derive from sites throughout Egypt. Sylvie Honigman has argued that regional differences play an important role in explaining the diverse cultural responses of various Judean communities throughout Hellenistic Egypt, including language (Honigman 2009). It seems likely that the shift from Aramaic to Greek did not occur among all the Judean communities of Egypt at the same time or at the same rate, with some retaining Aramaic significantly later than others.[28]

5.1.3 Elsewhere in the Hellenistic World

A dearth of Early Hellenistic epigraphic remains associated with Judeans from anywhere outside of Judea and Egypt precludes any substantive discussion about the spread of Greek among Judean communities elsewhere in the Hellenistic world. Susan Sherwin-White (1987: 24) has described how Aramaic, the lingua

---

[28] The "Nash Papyrus," a Hebrew text from Egypt dated paleographically to the late second century BCE and that includes Deut 5:6–21 (18), 6:3b (as per the Septuagint), 4–5, suggests that Hebrew was used – at least for ritual purposes – well into the Late Hellenistic period. See (*CPJ* 4, no. 609).

franca of the Achaemenid Empire, continued to be used for public inscriptions, administrative and legal records, and official communications in Babylonia and elsewhere in the Hellenistic east under the Seleucids. It is not unreasonable to conjecture that Aramaic continued to be used by most Judean communities in the east as well, even if some of their more elite members may have learned a certain amount of Greek to enable interactions with the Seleucid administration and perhaps also to facilitate interregional trade.

5.2 Greek Names

5.2.1 Judea

The Judean onomasticon from the Southern Levant compiled by Tal Ilan (2002) contains the names of forty-eight individuals recorded in Early Hellenistic inscriptions on papyri, ostraca and coins. All of these names are either Hebrew or Aramaic, with the exception of two Greek names borne by slaves: Eudomus and Ocimon (Ilan 2002: 278, 313; both are recorded in *CPJ* 1, no. 4). The only reason these two are identified as possibly Judean, however, is due to the fact that the slaves are said to be circumcised, and, as Tcherikover has already noted, male circumcision was practiced at this time by many of the peoples in the region (Tcherikover 1957: 127). Removing these names from the list leads to the conclusion that no inscriptional evidence has survived which might indicate the use of Greek personal names in Judea anytime during the century and a half after the conquests of Alexander the Great.

5.2.2 Egypt

In stark contrast to the situation in Judea, in Egypt Greek names appear to have proliferated among Judeans as early as the third century BCE. The Judean onomasticon from the western diaspora compiled by Ilan (2008) contains 355 male names identified as belonging to Judeans in Early Hellenistic Egypt: 58 percent are Hebrew (or otherwise Semitic), 35 percent are Greek, and the remainder mostly Egyptian.[29] Of the 41 female names identified as belonging to Judeans, 63 percent are Hebrew (or otherwise Semitic), 27 percent are Greek, and the remainder mostly Egyptian. As Tcherikover (1957: 28) and Ilan (2008: 3) have noted, however, Hebrew names are probably overrepresented in this onomasticon because often they are the sole marker of an individual's Judean identity – whereas other indicators are necessary to identify as Judean an

---

[29] These data include only names recorded on papyri, ostraca, and stone inscriptions, and that date to the Early Hellenistic period (332–175 BCE). I have included here names which Ilan has dated to "3rd–2nd century BCE." Names preserved in literary sources were not included.

individual bearing a Greek name. It seems likely, therefore, that Greek names were even more popular than the statistics above would imply. It is important to note, however, that Hebrew and Greek names continued to live side by side within families, such that a father might have a Hebrew name and his son a Greek name, or vice versa, and one spouse might have a Hebrew name and the other a Greek.

Honigman has noted that the adoption of Greek names among Judeans was more pronounced in some regions of Egypt than in others (Honigman 2009). Specifically, she noted a tendency within communities in Upper Egypt to continue to use Hebrew and Aramaic names that had been prevalent during the Persian period, well into the third and even second centuries BCE. As with the adoption of the Greek language, it seems likely that the adoption of Greek names did not occur among all the Judean communities of Egypt at the same time or at the same rate.

5.2.3 Elsewhere in the Hellenistic World

Outside of Judea and Egypt, the number of individuals identified as Judeans in inscriptions is far too small to draw any conclusions about naming conventions.

5.3 Greek Material Culture

Because it is difficult to identify uninscribed, Early Hellenistic archaeological remains unearthed outside of Judea as belonging to Judeans (see above, Section 1.4.1), we are compelled to limit our discussion about the adoption of Greek material culture among Judeans to archaeological data from Judea proper. In what follows, I will focus on pottery and architecture, two elements of material culture which are abundant, generally easy to identify as Greek-inspired, and relatively simple to date.

5.3.1 Pottery

In antiquity, pottery represented one of the most ubiquitous components of any given social group's material culture. Choices between different ceramic forms reflect not only aesthetic preferences, but also the varying ways that food was prepared, served, and consumed. The appearance of new ceramic forms, therefore, often reveals the adoption of novel cuisines and modes of dining.

Beginning in the Persian period and well into the Early Hellenistic period, trading ties with Athens led to the importation of Attic pottery at sites throughout the Southern Levant. The distribution pattern of these Hellenic imports into the region was uneven, however, as they are far more common at urban centers such as ʿAkko/Ptolemais, Dor, Samaria, and Maresha, and rare in rural areas like Judea (Rosenthal-Heginbottom 2015: 673).

Soon after the Macedonian conquests, potters in the north and along the coast began to produce local forms of dining, drinking, serving, and cooking vessels closely resembling Attic imports (Figure 13). In the central highlands, however, potters continued throughout the third century BCE to produce forms which largely resembled the local, Persian-era ceramic repertoire. It was only in the early second century BCE that Greek-styled pottery began to be produced in the region of Samaria, and it was not until the end of this century or the beginning of the next that these forms began to be produced in Judea (Berlin 2015: 629).

Worthy of particular attention is the casserole, a vessel with a wide mouth and body, and with a rounded bottom designed for stewing meat, fish, and vegetables (Figure 14). Andrea Berlin has argued compellingly that the novel appearance of casseroles at Levantine sites represents the adoption of a new, particularly Greek-styled cuisine centered on stewed dishes (Berlin 1993: 41–42). Elsewhere, she has noted that casseroles began to appear in the late third century BCE "everywhere" throughout the Southern Levant *except for in Judea*, where the form begins to appear only in the early first century BCE (Berlin 2015: 636). This differential distribution of casseroles may suggest that Judeans were quite late in adopting Greek-styled cooking practices compared with other Levantine groups.

5.3.2 Architectural Decorative Elements

Ancient Greek architecture famously emphasized decorative elements classified according to the three classical architectural orders: Doric, Ionian, and Corinthian. While these decorative elements were widely incorporated in the design of temples, gateways, colonnades (stoas), and other public buildings and monuments, their vocabulary also influenced the architecture and interior designs of more private structures like high-status homes and tombs. Archaeological remains of these elements primarily consist of bases, shafts, and capitals of columns and antae, various components of entablatures (architraves, friezes, and cornices), as well as pediment and roof decorations. Usually, even quite fragmentary remains can be identified as belonging to Greek-styled architectural decorations, and these can oftentimes be dated stylistically (even when found outside a stratigraphic context).

One of the earliest sites in the Southern Levant to boast Greek-style architectural decoration (albeit mixed with eastern elements) is at ʿIrāq al-Amīr in the Transjordan, in the early-to-mid-second century BCE Qasr al-ʿAbd structure commonly identified as belonging to the Judean Tobiad family

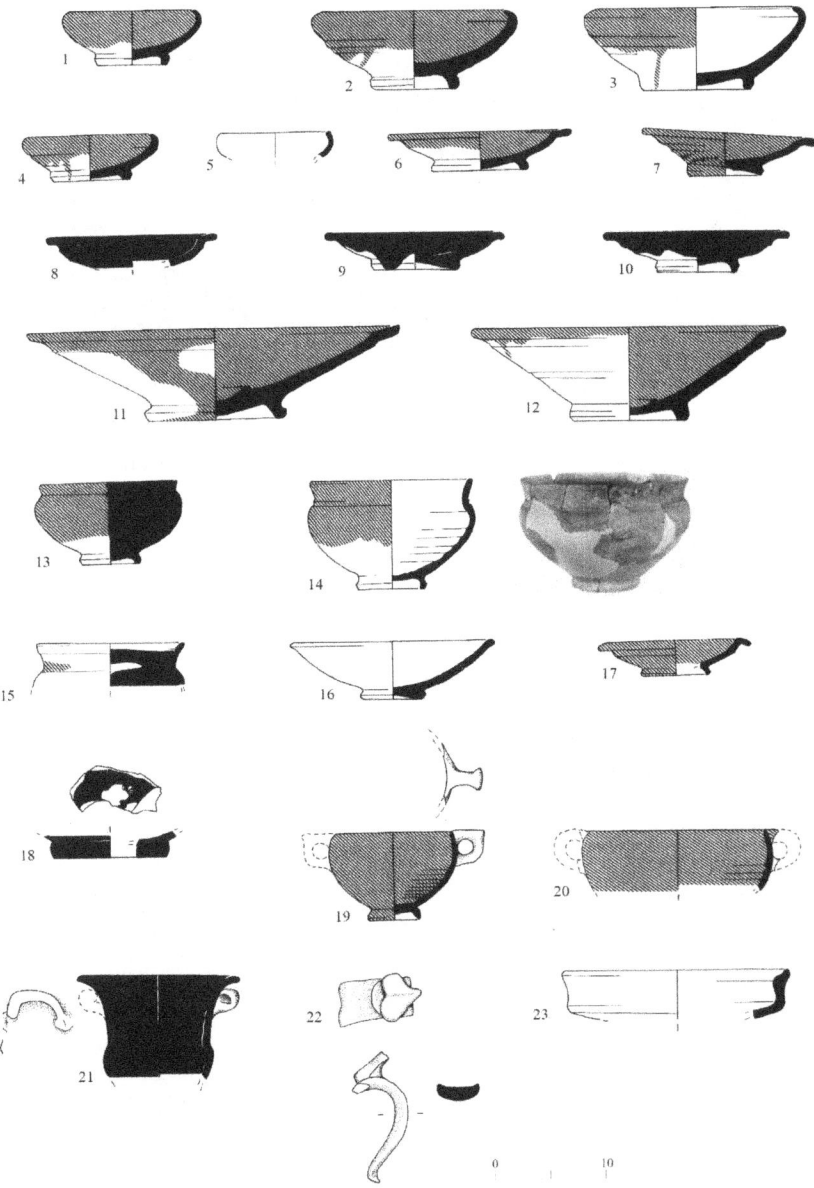

Figure 13 Ceramic bowls (1–10, 13–18), fish plates (11–12), skyphoi (19–20), kantharoi (21–22), and an open vessel/lid (23) from ʿAkko/Ptolemais; third century BCE (from: Smithline 2013: 75, Fig. 5. Courtesy of the IAA).

(Dentzer-Feydy 1991) (Figure 15). In a detailed survey of architectural decoration in Cisjordan during the Hellenistic period, Moshe Fischer and Oren Tal argued that the middle of the second century BCE marks the beginning of

Figure 14 Ceramic casserole from Tel Anafa, used for preparation of Greek-styled cuisine; Late Hellenistic but typical from the late third century BCE (Photo: courtesy of Sharon Herbert, Kedesh excavations).

Figure 15 Reconstructed west side of the Qasr al-ʿAbd structure (at ʿIrāq al-Amīr in the Transjordan) showing cornice decorated with Greek-style dentils, surmounted by an eastern-style lion sculpture; early to mid second century BCE (Photo: Yonatan Adler).

when such elements begin to appear in the region (Fischer and Tal 2003). They found this to be true not only of Judea, but also of non-Judean sites like Beth She'an/Scythopolis, Samaria, Gerizim, and Maresha. A more recent assessment by Orit Peleg-Barkat added meager new finds from Dor and Maresha dating to the third century BCE, but still nothing in Judea (Peleg-Barkat 2017). It seems that the absorption of Greek-styled architectural decoration into South Levantine architectural conventions was a slow process which only began to take root in earnest in the second and first centuries BCE.

5.4 Conclusions

In the previous section (Section 4.2.1), we surveyed evidence of Athena motifs on coins minted in Judea toward the end of the fourth century BCE. While this might suggest a certain openness to Greek influence in the Judean homeland early in the Hellenistic period, the data analyzed in the present section suggests that it would take some time before such an impact was to be felt in the spheres of language, naming conventions, pottery and architecture. By comparison, Judeans in Egypt seem to have more readily adopted Greek language and names already in the third century BCE. Even in Egypt, however, adoption of these cultural elements seems less a matter of rejecting traditional Judean culture in favor of Greek, and more about the very practical need to enable efficient communication and to facilitate social and commercial contacts with an increasingly Greek-speaking environment. As Honigman has argued, the fact the Judeans at Herakleopolis had almost exclusively Greek names while at the same time they conducted legal procedures in accordance with their ancestral Judean laws (see Section 2.2) suggests that adoption of Greek names and language does not necessarily imply wide-ranging cultural assimilation (Honigman 2009: 135).

Knowledge of Greek would have been a prerequisite to any kind of proficiency in Greek literature. In places where Judeans had yet to speak and read extensively in Greek, we must assume that the literature which was well-known and widely circulating would have been written in either Hebrew or Aramaic. In the following section, we will investigate what that literature might have been.

6 Literary Reception

Literature can play a powerful cultural role, even in societies whose members are mostly illiterate. The stories, poetry, wise advice, and other content embedded in literary texts may circulate widely in oral form alongside the written. These can have a pervasive impact on the values, beliefs and practices of the society in which they are widely shared. Because of this influence, a culture can experience profound transformation when previously unknown or unappreciated literary texts begin to enjoy widespread reception.

In the present section, we will inquire as to what literature might have been well-known and influential within Judean society during the Early Hellenistic period. If we can identify any such literature, we will investigate whether its circulation continues previous trends of reception or if any of it was new to the period. As most of the texts in what later came to be known as the Hebrew Bible were probably already composed by this time, we will begin our investigation by examining the possibility of widespread reception of these texts during the Early Hellenistic period. Following this, we will examine the possible reception of nonbiblical literature within Judean communities at this time.

6.1 Biblical Texts

In Section 3, we investigated possible widespread observance of the Torah, which is predicated on the legal portions of the Pentateuch. Here we will seek to identify the possible widespread reception of other biblical texts or traditions by examining three sorts of evidence: (1) citation of material from the Hebrew Bible in literary sources penned during the Early Hellenistic period; (2) biblical manuscripts that might date to the Early Hellenistic period; and (3) names of biblical heroes in the Judean onomasticon of personal names from this time.

6.1.1 Citation by Early Hellenistic Authors

Familiarity with heroes of the Hebrew Bible and with some of the stories associated with them is evident in several Judean literary texts whose composition many scholars date to the Early Hellenistic period. The most well-dated of these is the Wisdom of Joshua Ben Sira, which was probably first composed sometime around the first quarter of the second century BCE (Williams 1994). Its author referred to such Biblical figures as Adam (Sir 49:16), Seth (Sir 49:16), Enosh (Sir 49:16), Enoch (Sir 44:16; 49:14), Noah (Sir 44:17–18), Shem (Sir 49:16), Abraham, Isaac and Jacob (Sir 44:19–23), Joseph (49:15), Moses (Sir 24:23; 44:23–45:1–6, 15; 46:1, 7), Aaron (Sir 36:17; 45:6–22, 25), Phinehas (Sir 45:23–26), Joshua (Sir 46:1–6), Caleb (Sir 46:7–10), Samuel (Sir 46:13–20), Nathan (Sir 47:1), David (Sir 45:25; 47:1–11, 22; 48:15, 22; 49:4), Solomon (Sir 47:12–23), Rehoboam and Jeroboam (Sir 47:23–25), Elijah (Sir 48:1–12), Elisha (Sir 48:12–14), Hezekiah (Sir 48:17–22; 49:4), Isaiah (Sir 48:20–25), Josiah (Sir 49:1–4), Jeremiah (Sir 49:6–7), Ezekiel (Sir 49:8), Job (Sir 49:9), "the Twelve Prophets" (Sir 49:10), Zerubbabel and Jeshua, son of Jozadak (Sir 49:11–12), and Nehemiah (Sir 49:13).

Among other Judean works that many scholars date to the Early Hellenistic period and that betray a certain familiarity with biblical texts, we may mention Tobit, early sections of the so-called Enochic literature, the book of Giants, and the Aramaic Levi Document (see Grabbe 2008a: 81–84, 94–96, 98–100) along with several works found at Qumran (Lange 2006). Acquaintance with biblical figures and stories is also apparent in surviving fragments from the Greek writings of Demetrius the Chronographer, Ezekiel the Tragedian, and Artapanus (see Grabbe 2008a: 84–86, 89–92). In this category, we should also consider texts (or textual strata) in the Hebrew Bible itself which some scholars date to the Early Hellenistic period and that reflect knowledge of earlier material from elsewhere in the Hebrew Bible (see Schmid 2021). Finally, if we accept that the initial production of the Septuagint translation of the Pentateuch took place during the third century BCE as is commonly thought (Lee 1983; Dorival 1988: 55–58), it goes without saying that its translators were in possession of this biblical compilation, at the very least.

To what extent can such textual references teach us about widespread familiarity with the biblical texts themselves or with oral traditions associated with material incorporated in the Hebrew Bible? We must recall that producers of literature like the Early Hellenistic sources cited above were hardly representative of the general population within which these authors lived and worked. These were clearly highly literate individuals, capable of creating sophisticated literary works. The fact that they sometimes made use of biblical texts or traditions is certainly important for understanding what occupied the interests of Judean literati of the age. But it remains an open question how relevant such literary uses might be for understanding how much the *Judean masses* knew about these biblical texts or traditions.

6.1.2 Early Hellenistic Period Biblical Manuscripts

The earliest surviving manuscripts of texts which later came to be incorporated into the Hebrew Bible were discovered in the caves surrounding Qumran. The official publications of these texts usually included a paleographic analysis that assigned a date range for each manuscript (for bibliographic references, see Webster 2002: 371, 378–79).[30] The earliest paleographic dates, ranging from the middle of the third century until the first quarter of the second century BCE, were assigned to fragments from five scrolls representing the following biblical books: Exodus (4Q15), Exodus-Leviticus (4Q417), Deuteronomy (4Q46), Samuel (4Q52), and Jeremiah (4Q70). Another three scrolls were assigned paleographic dates between the late third century until 150 BCE: manuscripts of Genesis (6Q1), Leviticus (6Q2), and Job (4Q101). Five more scrolls were assigned a paleographic date range between 200 and 150 BCE: manuscripts of Leviticus (4Q249 j), of Deuteronomy in Hebrew (5Q1) and Greek (4Q122), and of Jeremiah (4Q71 and 4Q72a). None of these dates should be regarded as certain, however, as Frank Moore Cross has noted with regard to the paleographic dating

---

[30] For a slightly different list of "pre-Maccabean" biblical texts from Qumran, see Lange 2006.

of scripts thought to predate the Hasmonean era: "The dating of documents in the Archaic or proto-Jewish period (ca. 250–150 BC) is less precise, still being largely based on typological sequence" (Cross 1961: 135).

Approximately thirty of the Dead Sea Scrolls were subjected to radiocarbon dating in the 1990s. Among the few biblical texts in this small group, none provided results suggesting that they were likely to have been produced during the Early Hellenistic period (for an overview and updated calibration dates, see Doudna 1998).

A more recent study subjected an additional thirty Dead Sea Scrolls manuscripts to radiocarbon dating, and then used these texts to train an artificial intelligence-based data-prediction model to paleographically date similar scripts found on other Dead Sea Scrolls manuscripts (Popović et al. 2024). Among the Biblical scrolls assigned radiocarbon dates, manuscripts of Samuel (4Q52) and Jeremiah (4Q70) were found with a high degree of confidence (95 percent) to date to the third or perhaps even fourth century BCE (as noted above, both of these scrolls had been assigned Early Hellenistic-period paleographic dates as well). A Deuteronomy manuscript (4Q30) was radiocarbon dated to the mid fourth to early second century BCE with the same likelihood.[31] The study's artificial intelligence model predicted a 300 to 240 BCE date for an Ecclesiastes manuscript (4Q109).

Assuming that some of the biblical manuscripts from the Qumran caves were indeed penned during the Early Hellenistic period, the question remains what the existence of such manuscripts at Qumran has to teach us about the likelihood that these compositions were widely known among the general populace. The Qumran assemblage appears to have been owned and used by a unique group of pietist sectarians who flourished during the Hasmonean and Herodian periods. If members of this group were not representative of their own contemporaries, the same may have been true of those who bequeathed to them these early manuscripts.

6.1.3 Names of Biblical Heroes in the Judean Onomasticon

A survey of Judean names preserved in the rather extensive epigraphic record from the Early Hellenistic period in both Judea and the diaspora indicates that very few names used by Judeans at the time coincided with names of heroes from the biblical tradition (Ilan 2002, 2008).[32] Within a surviving set of 412 male

---

[31] A scroll containing text from Daniel 10–11 (4Q114) was assigned a similar radiocarbon date, but the authors of the study prefer the later end of this range since biblical scholars usually date the composition of this text to the 160s BCE on literary-historical grounds.

[32] I have culled the data presented here from the corpora assembled by Ilan from Judea (Ilan 2002) and the western diaspora, including Egypt (Ilan 2008). These data include only names recorded

names, only one individual bears the name Abraham (in Hebrew as *'avrām*), another individual is named Jacob (in Greek as Iakkóbios), two are named Judah, and one is named Aaron, (in Greek as Árōn). Names of central figures like Isaac, Moses, Joshua, and David are not represented at all. Figures who are far less central to the biblical tradition, like Simon, Joseph, and Jonathan, do appear somewhat more frequently within this Judean onomasticon – especially in Egypt – but this fact hardly necessitates that the Biblical tradition was already circulating widely at this time.[33] Within a surviving set of forty-three female names, central female characters from the Hebrew Bible are represented only by Sarah (twice) and Miriam (three times).

It is important to note here that even in subsequent centuries, during the Late Hellenistic period and well into the Roman era, names of biblical heroes remain uncommon in the Judean onomasticon (Ilan 2002: 5–6). Although it seems quite likely that during these later periods the central protagonists of the biblical tradition were already well known among Judeans at large, even *then* the convention of naming children after these figures had apparently yet to take root. With this in mind, we should probably not read too much into the dearth of names of biblical heroes among Judeans in the Early Hellenistic period either.

6.2 Nonbiblical Literature

An Aramaic manuscript of the Words of Aḥiqar was discovered among the papyri of Elephantine and dated to the fifth century BCE (*TAD*, C1.1). Scholars commonly regard this papyrus as part of the Judean collection of documents, although its actual connection with the Judean community remains uncertain (Kratz 2022: 301–3). Regardless, the fact that the Book of Tobit presents a Judean version of the story of Aḥiqar as part of its own narrative suggests that the work had a certain amount of circulation among Judeans well into the Hellenistic period when Tobit is thought to have been composed (Kratz 2022: 316–18). While it is hard to infer from any of this how *widespread* the reception of Aḥiqar might have been among Judean communities in the Early Hellenistic period, the very fact that we know of its existence around this time is significant. If it is only by the chance preservation at Elephantine and in Tobit that we know anything at all about the reception of Aḥiqar among Judeans, it stands to reason that other literary works that have since been entirely lost were similarly in circulation among Judeans around this time.

---

on papyri, ostraca, coins, and stone inscriptions, and that date to the Early Hellenistic period (332–175 BCE). I have included names which Ilan has dated to "3rd–2nd century BCE." Names preserved in literary sources were not included.

[33] These names appear already before the start of the Early Hellenistic period, but rarely; see Zadok 1988.

Beyond this inferential observation, very little hard evidence has survived for the reception of nonbiblical literary works among Judean communities during the Early Hellenistic period. A fragment of a calendrical text entitled "4QAstronomical Enoch^a ar" (4Q208) has been dated paleographically to the end of the third or beginning of the second century BCE (Webster 2002: 378), but the scroll has been radiocarbon dated slightly later (Doudna 1998: 470). And a fragment of the Testament of Qahat preserved at Qumran (4Q542) has been radiocarbon dated with a high degree of confidence (95 percent) to before 181 BCE (Doudna 1998: 468), but its script has been dated paleographically to the last quarter of the second century BCE (Webster 2002: 365) or even later (Popović et al. 2024). No other nonbiblical literary manuscripts from the Judean Desert have been dated to the Early Hellenistic period.

It is often thought that many of the nonbiblical works discovered at Qumran were first composed prior to the Maccabean revolt (Lange 2006). As noted above (Section 6.1.1), many scholars date to the Early Hellenistic period the composition of works such as Tobit, early sections of the so-called Enochic literature, the Book of Giants, and the Aramaic Levi Document, as well as the Greek writings of Demetrius the Chronographer, Ezekiel the Tragedian, and Artapanus. How widespread the reception of any of these literary works might have been among Judean communities in the Early Hellenistic period, however, remains essentially unknown.

We are similarly in the dark as to the extent to which Judeans in Greek-speaking areas like Egypt might have been familiar with Greek literature. Works of classical authors such as Homer, Euripides, Plato, and Thucydides have been found on Egyptian papyri dating to the early or mid third century BCE (Turner 1968: 107), but none of these have been associated with Judean communities.

6.3 Conclusions

There is little evidence to suggest that traditions surrounding what later came to be known as the Hebrew Bible were already circulating widely in the Early Hellenistic period. It seems quite possible that Reinhard Kratz is correct in his intriguing assessment that, prior to the Hasmonean period, much of the Biblical tradition was probably circulating among only limited and marginal circles of intellectuals, perhaps those associated with small scribal schools (Kratz 2015: 184–87, 196, 197–200; 2024). While it stands to reason that ordinary Judeans in the Early Hellenistic era did in fact engage with traditions preserved in literary works of various sorts – as the Judeans of Elephantine appear to have done in the Persian era – the identity and character of these texts remain largely unknown to us today. Whatever these literary texts might have been, there is little reason to assume that their reception at this time was novel in a way that might have been transformative of Judean society.

7 Conclusions

This study set out to investigate the character of Judean cult and culture during the Early Hellenistic period, as a transitional time between the preceding Persian era and the subsequent Late Hellenistic and Roman periods. Specifically, we sought to determine the degree to which this era might have been one of cultural continuity with the Yahwism of the past, versus the degree to which it might have been characterized by cultural rupture with the emergence of something like the nascent Judaism that came to be known in the ensuing eras. Our focus has been on Judean society at large, represented primarily by the masses of common people who composed the majority of the population – rather than on any small number of nonrepresentative Judean literati.

We have seen that during the Early Hellenistic period, Judeans appear to have enjoyed significant semi-autonomous authority in political, cultic, and possibly also legal matters, both in the administration of the province of Judea, as well as in the organization of at least some Judean communities abroad. In important ways, this appears to be a carryover from policies of the Achaemenid Empire, which permitted a significant degree of self-governance among Judeans (among its other denizens), subordinate to imperial rule. In Judea proper, while the office of governor seems to disappear at some stage, the central role of the Judean high priest that emerged in the Persian period continued to play a dominant role throughout Ptolemaic and early Seleucid rule. If Judeans were adjudicating themselves under their own sets of laws, however, we lack the data to be able to identify or characterize any such bodies of regulations. Crucially, there is little reason to assume that the Torah, predicated on Pentateuchal legislation, had already come to be widely known and recognized as authoritative at this early stage. Like the Persian period, the Early Hellenistic period has produced none of the material or textual evidence indicating widespread Torah observance as we have from the Late Hellenistic and Roman periods.

Judeans of the Early Hellenistic period clearly inherited from their forebears the longstanding tradition of venerating YHWH as their primary deity, a tradition that reaches as far back as the Iron Age (if not earlier). The same YHWH temple in Jerusalem which had apparently been established in the Persian period (probably on Iron Age foundations) appears to have continued to function uninterruptedly throughout the Hellenistic period and into the start of the Roman period. There also appear to be certain indications, albeit somewhat speculative, that the noncentralized, nonexclusive Yahwism of the Iron

Age and Persian era continued to characterize Judean cult well into the Early Hellenistic period. This includes hints that Judeans may have continued to conduct cultic worship of YHWH at sites located outside of Jerusalem. It also includes certain indications that Judeans, to one degree or another, continued to venerate other deities alongside YHWH.

In Judea, we find a strong degree of cultural continuity from the preceding Persian period in terms of language (Aramaic), naming conventions, and material culture – with almost no evidence for Greek influence in these matters. In Egypt, by contrast, Judeans began to replace Aramaic with Greek, and began to adopt Greek names alongside traditional Hebrew and Aramaic names. However, as the trigger for both these developments in Egypt was likely the very practical need to facilitate social and commercial contacts in an increasingly Greek-speaking environment, we should probably not regard these shifts as a fundamental rejection of traditional Judean culture in favor of Greek.

While most of the literature that later came to constitute the Hebrew Bible is thought to have been initially composed prior to the Early Hellenistic period, we know almost nothing about the reception of various elements of this literary material with Judean society at large at this time. As in the Persian period, there is little reason to think that either this literature or the oral traditions associated with it were circulating widely among the masses in the Early Hellenistic period. We similarly know close to nothing about the circulation of other, nonbiblical literary traditions among Judeans at this time. There is little reason to think that this period marks a time when a novel reception of *any* literary texts – Biblical or otherwise – might have been transformative of Judean society.

From all the above, it appears that the Early Hellenistic period represents a time of marked cultural continuity with the preceding Persian period. While the march of time would have inevitably led to certain incremental developments in the cult and culture of the Judeans, there is little if any reason to regard the Early Hellenistic period as one of cultural rupture. If it is preferable to speak of "Yahwism" rather than "Judaism" when discussing the Persian period, we should probably retain this preference when discussing the Early Hellenistic period as well.[34]

---

[34] For a similar assessment of continuity with regard to the material cultural of the entire Southern Levant (not just Judea), see Tal 2006, especially p. 335: "The history of settlement and social history reflected in the archaeological data evinces 'continuity' rather than 'rupture'" (my translation from the Hebrew). Recently, Nitsan Shalom and others have concluded that various regions of Judea underwent significant shifts in their settlement patterns during the transition between the Persian and Early Hellenistic periods (Shalom et al. 2021). Whatever the causes of these changes, they do not appear to have had much of an impact on the elements of cult and culture examined here.

Following the close of the Early Hellenistic period, the next two and a half centuries witnessed revolutionary developments within Judean society. Less than a decade after the death of Seleucus IV, the Maccabean uprising erupted under the command of the Hasmoneans, ultimately leading to political independence and the founding of the first fully sovereign Judean polity since the fall of Jerusalem in 586 BCE. From a semi-autonomous province, Judea became a fully autonomous commonwealth. At the head of this new state stood the high priest, who now became the concurrent cultic, political, and military leader of the nation. Upon the heels of the revolutionary founding of this new regime, we increasingly come to encounter evidence of widespread Torah observance, which developed into the Judeans' "ancestral law," and which came to regulate innumerable aspects of daily life both in the homeland and abroad. The Torah appears to have been made into the law of the land throughout the Southern Levant, not only for Judeans themselves, but also for the Semitic neighbors they conquered: Idumeans, Samaritans, and Itureans. Judeans' worship came to be centered exclusively on a single deity, and the Jerusalem temple developed into the sole legitimate site for sacrificial worship and pilgrimage.[35] The development of Jerusalem's status as cultic center is clearly manifest in the rebuilding of its temple compound by Herod the Great toward the end of the first century BCE, and in the exponential growth of the city throughout the Hasmonean and Herodian eras as evidenced in the archaeological record. As Judea moved from the status of a provincial backwater to that of an independent state, and as it began to act as a player on the stage of the larger Hellenistic world, Greek language, naming conventions, and material culture began to make significant inroads even in the ancestral homeland. And during this time, texts and traditions associated with what eventually became our Hebrew Bible came to achieve widespread reception among Judean communities virtually everywhere they were found. The Hasmonean and Herodian eras present a clear watershed in the transformative development of Judean cult and culture. For the first time ever, the basic framework of Judaism as we know it finally comes fully into view.

At this point, it bears asking how the century and a half following the conquests of Alexander the Great might have set the stage for the seismic shifts to come. Until new data from archaeology, papyrology, epigraphy, and numismatics become available, we can answer this question in only general terms. The semiautonomous power assumed by the office of the high priest in the Persian and Early Hellenistic eras clearly established the framework for the fully autonomous Hasmonean political regime that followed. Furthermore,

---

[35] A YHWH temple was established in Leontopolis (in Lower Egypt) near the start of this period, but this should probably be seen as a carryover from the Early Hellenistic era. This temple never enjoyed the widespread legitimacy of the Jerusalem temple. See also Kasher 1985: 119–35.

the Early Hellenistic period was the time when much of what later came to be known as the Biblical tradition was passed down, although we can only guess as to the mechanisms behind the transmission of this literature. We might conjecture, along with Kratz (see above, Section 6.3), that at this time the Pentateuch and other parts of the biblical tradition were circulating among limited circles of pietists whose marginal views later came to win the day under Hasmonean aegis. These traditions would have laid the groundwork for the Judean cult eventually homing its focus entirely onto a single deity to be worshiped in a single temple. In these ways, while the Early Hellenistic period certainly appears to mark a strong degree of continuity with the Yahwism of the past, in some senses it may also be thought to have paved the way for the subsequent transition into the Judaism of the future.

Abbreviations

Standard abbreviations are followed for names of ancient sources (e.g., Bible, Apocrypha, Pseudepigrapha, Dead Sea Scrolls, Josephus, and classical and ancient Christian writings).

CIIP	*Corpus Inscriptionum Iudaeae/Palaestinae* (vol. 1: Cotton et al. 2010–12; vol. 4: Ameling et al. 2018)
CJZC	*Corpus jüdischer Zeugnisse aus der Cyrenaika* (Lüderitz 1983)
CPJ	*Corpus Papyrorum Judaicarum* (vols. 1–3: Tcherikover 1957–1964; vol. 4: Hacham and Ilan 2020)
IJO	*Inscriptiones Judaicae Orientis* (Noy, Panayotov, and Bloedhorn 2004)
JIGRE	*Jewish Inscriptions of Graeco-Roman Egypt* (Horbury and Noy 1992)
OGIS	*Orientis Graeci Inscriptiones Selectae* (Dittenberger, 1903–1905)
SC	*Samarian Coinage* (Meshorer and Qedar 1999)
TAD	*Textbook of Aramaic Documents from Ancient Egypt* (Porten and Yardeni 1986–1999)
TJC	*A Treasury of Jewish Coins* (Meshorer 2001)
YC	*The Yehud Coinage* (Gitler, Lorber, and Fontanille 2023)
YSI	*The Yehud Stamp Impressions* (Lipschits and Vanderhooft 2011)

References

Adler, Y. (2022). *The Origins of Judaism: An Archaeological-Historical Reappraisal*. New Haven, CT: Yale University Press.

Adler, Y. (2025). "Toward Identifying Proto-Judaic Cultural Features in Ancient Israel and Judea." *Journal of Ancient Judaism* 16: 1–28. https://doi.org/10.30965/21967954-bja10069

Adler, Y., and O. Lernau. (2021). "The Pentateuchal Dietary Proscription against Finless and Scaleless Aquatic Species in Light of Ancient Fish Remains." *Tel Aviv* 48: 5–26.

Aharoni, Y. (1968). "Trial Excavation in the 'Solar Shrine' at Lachish Preliminary Report." *Israel Exploration Journal* 18: 157–169.

Aharoni, Y. (1975). *Investigations at Lachish: The Sanctuary and the Residency (Lachish V)*. Tel Aviv: Gateway.

Aḥituv, S., E. Eshel, and Z. Meshel. (2012). "The Inscriptions." In *Kuntillet ʿAjrud (Ḥorvat Teman): An Iron Age II Religious Site on the Judah-Sinai Border*, edited by Z. Meshel, 73–142. Jerusalem: Israel Exploration Society.

Albertz, R. (2001). "An End to the Confusion? Why the Old Testament Cannot Be a Hellenistic Book!" In *Did Moses Speak Attic? Jewish Historiography and Scripture in the Hellenistic Period*, edited by L. L. Grabbe, 30–46. Sheffield: Sheffield Academic.

Alstola, T. (2020). *Judeans in Babylonia: A Study of Deportees in the Sixth and Fifth Centuries BCE*. Leiden: Brill.

Altmann, P. (2021). "The Significance of the Divine Torah in Ptolemaic Egypt in Documentary and Literary Sources from the Third and Second Centuries BCE." *Journal for the Study of Judaism* 52: 1–31.

Ameling, W., H. M. Cotton, W. Eck et al. (2018). *Corpus Inscriptionum Iudaeae/Palaestinae, Volume IV: Iudaea/Idumaea. Parts 1–2*. Berlin: De Gruyter.

Avigad, N. (1976). *Bullae and Seals from a Post-Exilic Judean Archive*, translated by R. Grafman. Jerusalem: Institute of Archaeology, Hebrew University of Jerusalem.

Bar-Kochva, B. (1996). *Pseudo-Hecataeus, "On the Jews": Legitimizing the Jewish Diaspora*. Berkeley: University of California Press.

Bar-Kochva, B. (2010). *The Image of the Jews in Greek Literature*. Berkeley: University of California Press.

Barnea, G. (2021). *Khnum is against Us since Hananiah Has Been in Egypt: Yahwistic Reform and Identity in the Prism of Elephantine: 419–399 BCE*. PhD dissertation, University of Haifa.

Barnea, G. (2024). Yahwistic Identity in the Achaemenid Period. *Zeitschrift für die alttestamentliche Wissenschaft* 136 (1): 1–14.

Barnea, G., and R. Kratz, eds. (2024). *Yahwism under the Achaemenid Empire: Professor Shaul Shaked in Memoriam*. Berlin: De Gruyter.

Barr, J. (1989). "Hebrew, Aramaic and Greek in the Hellenistic Age." In *The Cambridge History of Judaism, Vol. 2, The Hellenistic Age*, edited by W. D. Davies and L. Finkelstein, 79–114. Cambridge: Cambridge University Press.

Becking, B. (2008). "Temples across the Border and the Communal Borders within Yahwistic Yehud." *Transeuphratène* 35: 39–54.

Berlin, A. M. (1993). "Italian Cooking Vessels and Cuisine at Tel Anafa." *Israel Exploration Journal* 43: 35–44.

Berlin, A. M. (2015). "Hellenistic Period." In *The Ancient Pottery of Israel and its Neighbors from the Iron Age through the Hellenistic Period, Vol. 2*, edited by S. Gitin, 629–671. Jerusalem: Israel Exploration Society.

Berthelot, K. (2008). "Hecataeus of Abdera and Jewish 'Misanthropy'" *Bulletin du Centre de recherche français à Jérusalem* 19. https://journals.openedition.org/bcrfj/5968.

Bianco, M., and C. Bonnet. (2016). "Sur les traces d'Athéna chez les Phéniciens." *Pallas* 100: 155–179.

Bickerman, E. J. (2007a). "The Seleucid Charter for Jerusalem." In *Studies in Jewish and Christian History*, edited by A. Tropper, 315–356. Leiden: Brill.

Bickerman, E. J. (2007b). "A Seleucid Proclamation Concerning the Temple in Jerusalem." In *Studies in Jewish and Christian History*, edited by A. Tropper, 357–375. Leiden: Brill.

Burton, A. (1972). *Diodorus Siculus, Book 1: A Commentary*. Leiden: Brill.

Cohen, S. J. D. (1999). *The Beginnings of Jewishness: Boundaries, Varieties, Uncertainties*. Berkeley: University of California Press.

Collins, J. J. (2017). *The Invention of Judaism: Torah and Jewish Identity from Deuteronomy to Paul*. Oakland: University of California Press.

Collins, J. J. (2024). "Hecataeus as a Witness to Judaism." In *A Vision of the Days: Studies in Early Jewish History and Historiography in Honor of Daniel R. Schwartz*, edited by R. Brody, N. Hacham, M. M. Piotrkowski, and J. W. Van Henten, 321–337. Leiden: Brill.

Cotton, H. M., L. Di Segni, W. Eck, et al., eds. (2010–2012). *Corpus Inscriptionum Iudaeae/Palaestinae, Volume I: Jerusalem. Parts 1–2*. Berlin: De Gruyter.

Cowey, James M. S., and Klaus Maresch. (2001). *Urkunden des Politeuma der Juden von Herakleopolis (144/3–133/2 v. Chr.) (P. Polit. Iud.): Papyri aus den Sammlungen von Heidelberg, Köln, München und Wien*. Wiesbaden: Westdeutscher Verlag.

References

Cross, F. M. (1961). "The Development of Jewish Scripts." In *The Bible and the Ancient Near East: Essays in Honor of William Foxwell Albright*, edited by G. E. Wright, 133–202. Garden City, NY: Doubleday.

Cross, F. M. (1981). "An Aramaic Ostracon of the Third Century B.C.E. from Excavations in Jerusalem." *Eretz-Israel* 15: 67*–69*.

Dentzer-Feydy, J. (1991). "Le décor architectural." In *'Iraq al Amir: Le château du Tobiade Hyrcan*, edited by E. Will and F. Larché, 141–208. Paris: Librairie Orientaliste Paul Geuthner.

Derfler, S. (1993). *The Hellenistic Temple at Tel Beersheva*. Lewiston, NY: Mellen Press.

de Wette, W. M. L. (1813). *Lehrbuch der christlichen Dogmatik, in ihrer historischen Entwickelung dargestellt*. Vol. 1, *Biblische Dogmatik Alten und Neuen Testaments. Oder kritische Darstellung der Religionslehre des Hebraismus, des Judenthums und Urchristenthums*. Berlin: Realschulbuchhandlung.

Dittenberger, W. (1903–1905). *Orientis graeci inscriptiones selectae. Supplementum Sylloges inscriptionum graecarum*. Leipzig: S. Hirzel.

Dorival, G. (1988). "Les origines de la Septante: La traduction en grec des cinq livres de la Torah." In *La Bible grecque des Septante: du judaïsme hellénistique au christianisme ancien*, edited by G. Dorival, M. Harl, and O. Munnich, 39–82. Paris: Cerf/C.N.R.S.

Doudna, G. (1998). "Dating the Scrolls on the Basis of Radiocarbon Analysis." In *The Dead Sea Scrolls after Fifty Years: A Comprehensive Assessment*. Vol. 1, edited by P. W. Flint and J. C. VanderKam, 430–471. Leiden: Brill.

Eshel, H., and Misgav, H. (2000). "Jericho papList of Loans ar." In *Miscellaneous Texts from the Judaean Desert*, edited by J. Charlesworth, N. Cohen, H. Cotton et al. in consultation with J. VanderKam and M. Brady, 21–30. Discoveries in the Judaean Desert 38. Oxford: Clarendon.

Finkelstein, I. (2018). *Hasmonean Realities behind Ezra, Nehemiah, and Chronicles*. Atlanta, GA: Society of Biblical Literature.

Fischer, M., and O. Tal. (2003). "Architectural Decoration in Ancient Israel in Hellenistic Times: Some Aspects of Hellenization." *Zeitschrift des Deutschen Palästina-Vereins* 119 (1): 19–37.

Fontanille, J.-P., and C. C. Lorber. (2008). "Silver *Yehud* Coins with Greek or Pseudo-Greek Inscriptions." *Israel Numismatic Research* 3: 45–49.

Fraser, P. M. (1972). *Ptolemaic Alexandria*. Oxford: Clarendon.

Frevel, C., K. Pyschny, and I. Cornelius, eds. (2014). *A "Religious Revolution" in Yehûd? The Material Culture of the Persian Period as a Test Case*. Fribourg: Academic Press; Göttingen: Vandenhoeck & Ruprecht.

Gera, D. (2009). "Olympiodoros, Heliodoros and the Temples of Koilē Syria and Phoinikē." *Zeitschrift für Papyrologie und Epigraphik* 169: 125–155.

Gitler, H., C. Lorber, and J.-P. Fontanille. (2023). *The Yehud Coinage: A Study and Die Classification of the Provincial Silver Coinage of Judah.* Numismatic Studies and Researches 12. Jerusalem: Israel Numismatic Society.

Golub, M. R. (2023). "Onomasticon.net: Personal Names from the Iron II Southern Levant." Onomasticon.net. www.onomasticon.net/

Grabbe, L. L. (2001a). "Jewish Historiography and Scripture in the Hellenistic Period." In *Did Moses Speak Attic? Jewish Historiography and Scripture in the Hellenistic Period*, edited by L. L. Grabbe, 129–155. Sheffield: Sheffield Academic.

Grabbe, L. L. (2001b). "The Law of Moses in the Ezra Tradition: More Virtual than Real?" In *Persia and Torah: The Theory of Imperial Authorization of the Pentateuch*, edited by J. W. Watts, 91–113. Atlanta, GA: Scholars Press.

Grabbe, L. L. (2004). *A History of the Jews and Judaism in the Second Temple Period*. Vol. 1, *Yehud: A History of the Persian Province of Judah*. London: T&T Clark International.

Grabbe, L. L. (2008a). *A History of the Jews and Judaism in the Second Temple Period*. Vol. 2, *The Early Hellenistic Period (335–175 BCE)*. London: T&T Clark International.

Grabbe, L. L. (2008b). "Hecataeus of Abdera and the Jewish Law: The Question of Authenticity." In *Berührungspunkte: Studien zur Sozial-und Religionsgeschichte Israels und seiner Umwelt; Festschrift für Rainer Albertz zu seinem 65. Geburtstag*, edited by I. Kottsieper, R. Schmitt, and J. Wöhrle, 613–626. Münster: Ugarit-Verlag.

Grabbe, L. L. (2011). "Hyparchs, *Oikonomoi*, and Mafiosi: The Governance of Judah in the Ptolemaic Period." In *Judah between East and West: The Transition from Persian to Greek Rule (ca. 400–200 BCE)*, edited by L. L. Grabbe and O. Lipschits, 70–90. London: T&T Clark.

Grabbe, L. L. (2021). "The Ptolemaic Period: A Dark Age in Jewish History?" In *Times of Transition: Judea in the Early Hellenistic Period*, edited by S. Honigman, C. Nihan, and O. Lipschits, 19–30. University Park, PA: Eisenbrauns; Tel Aviv: Emery and Claire Yass Publications in Archaeology, the Institute of Archaeology, Tel Aviv University.

Granerød, G. (2016). *Dimensions of Yahwism in the Persian Period: Studies in the Religion and Society of the Judaean Community at Elephantine*. Berlin: De Gruyter.

Granerød, G. (2019). "Canon and Archive: Yahwism in Elephantine and Āl-Yāḫūdu as a Challenge to the Canonical History of Judean Religion in the Persian Period." *Journal of Biblical Literature* 138: 345–364.

Hacham, N., and T. Ilan, eds. (2020). *Corpus Papyrorum Judaicarum*. Vol. 4. Berlin: De Gruyter; Jerusalem: Magnes.

Hegermann, H. (1989). "The Diaspora in the Hellenistic Age." In *The Cambridge History of Judaism, Vol. 2, The Hellenistic Age*, edited by W. D. Davies, and L. Finkelstein, 115–166. Cambridge: Cambridge University Press.

Heinrichs, J. (2018). "Antiochos III and Ptolemy, Son of Thraseas, on Private Villages in Syria Koile Around 200 BC: The Hefzibah Dossier." *Zeitschrift für Papyrologie und Epigraphik* 206: 272–311.

Hengel, M. (1974). *Judaism and Hellenism: Studies in their Encounter in Palestine During the Early Hellenistic Period*. Vols. 1–2. Philadelphia: Fortress Press.

Honigman, S. (2009). "Jewish Communities of Hellenistic Egypt: Different Responses to Different Environments." In *Jewish Identities in Antiquity: Studies in Memory of Menahem Stern*, edited by L. I. Levine and D. R. Schwartz, 117–135. Tübingen: Mohr Siebeck.

Honigman, S., C. Nihan, and O. Lipschits, eds. (2021). *Times of Transition: Judea in the Early Hellenistic Period*. University Park, PA: Eisenbrauns; Tel Aviv: Emery and Claire Yass Publications in Archaeology, the Institute of Archaeology, Tel Aviv University.

Horbury, W., and D. Noy. (1992). *Jewish Inscriptions of Graeco-Roman Egypt: With an Index of the Jewish Inscriptions of Egypt and Cyrenaica*. New York: Cambridge University Press.

Ilan, T. (2002). *Lexicon of Jewish Names in Late Antiquity; Part I: Palestine 330 BCE–200 CE*. Tübingen: Mohr Siebeck.

Ilan, T. (2008). *Lexicon of Jewish Names in Late Antiquity; Part III: The Western Diaspora 330 BCE–650 CE*. Tübingen: Mohr Siebeck.

Jackson, K. P., and J. A. Dearman. (1989). "The Text of the Mesha' Inscription." In *Studies in the Mesha Inscription and Moab*, edited by A. Dearman, 93–95. Atlanta: Scholars.

Kasher, A. (1985). *The Jews in Hellenistic and Roman Egypt: The Struggle for Equal Rights*. Tübingen: J. C. B. Mohr.

Kasher, A. (2002). "Review of *Urkunden des Politeuma der Juden von Herakleopolis (144/3–133/2 v. Chr.) (P. Polit. Iud.): Papyri aus den Sammlungen von Heidelberg, Köln, München und Wien*, by J.M.S. Cowey and K. Maresch." *Jewish Quarterly Review* 93: 257–268.

Kratz, R. G. (2015). *Historical and Biblical Israel: The History, Tradition, and Archives of Israel and Judah*, translated by P. M. Kurtz. Oxford: Oxford University Press.

Kratz, R. G. (2020). "'Fossile Überreste des unreformierten Judentums in fernem Lande'? Das Judentum in den Archiven von Elephantine und Al-Yaḥudu." *Zeitschrift für die alttestamentliche Wissenschaft* 132: 23–39.

Kratz, R. G. (2021). "Greek Historians on Jews and Judaism in the 3rd Century BCE." In *Times of Transition: Judea in the Early Hellenistic Period*, edited by S. Honigman, C. Nihan, and O. Lipschits, 263–278. University Park, PA: Eisenbrauns; Tel Aviv: Emery and Claire Yass Publications in Archaeology, the Institute of Archaeology, Tel Aviv University.

Kratz, R. G. (2022). "Aḥiqar and Bisitun: The Literature of the Judeans at Elephantine." In *Elephantine in Context Studies on the History, Religion and Literature of the Judeans in Persian Period Egypt*, edited by R. G. Kratz and B. U. Schipper, 301–322. Tübingen: Mohr Siebeck.

Kratz, R. G. (2024). *"Väterliche Gesetze" und das Gesetz des Mose: Die Rolle der Tora im judäischen Aufstand gegen Antiochos IV.* Tübingen: Mohr Siebeck.

Kreimerman, I., and D. Sandhaus. (2021). "Political Trends as Reflected in the Material Culture: A New Look at the Transition between the Persian and Early Hellenistic Periods." In *Times of Transition: Judea in the Early Hellenistic Period*, edited by S. Honigman, C. Nihan, and O. Lipschits, 119–131. University Park, PA: Eisenbrauns; Tel Aviv: Emery and Claire Yass Publications in Archaeology, the Institute of Archaeology, Tel Aviv University.

Kuhs, C. (1996). *Das Dorf Samareia im griechisch-römischen Ägypten*. MA thesis, Institute for Papyrology, Heidelberg University.

Lange, A. (2006). "Pre-Maccabean Literature from the Qumran Library and the Hebrew Bible." *Dead Sea Discoveries* 13: 277–305.

Lee, J. A. L. (1983). *A Lexical Study of the Septuagint Version of the Pentateuch*. Chico: Scholars Press.

LeFebvre, M. (2006). *Collections, Codes, and Torah: The Re-characterization of Israel's Written Law*. New York: T&T Clark.

Lemaire, A. (2015). *Levantine Epigraphy and History in the Achaemenid Period (539–332 BCE)*. Oxford: Oxford University Press.

Lipschits, O. (2005). *The Fall and Rise of Jerusalem: Judah under Babylonian Rule*. Winona Lake: Eisenbrauns.

Lipschits, O. (2021). *Age of Empires: The History and Administration of Judah in the 8th–2nd Centuries BCE in Light of the Storage-Jar Stamp Impressions*.

University Park, PA: Eisenbrauns; Tel Aviv: The Institute of Archaeology, Tel Aviv University.

Lipschits, O., and O. Tal. (2007). "The Settlement Archaeology of the Province of Judah: A Case Study." In *Judah and the Judeans in the Fourth Century B.C.E.*, edited by O. Lipschits, G. N. Knoppers, and R. Albertz, 33–52. Winona Lake: Eisenbrauns.

Lipschits, O., and D. S. Vanderhooft. (2011). *The Yehud Stamp Impressions: A Corpus of Inscribed Impressions from the Persian and Hellenistic Periods in Judah*. Winona Lake: Eisenbrauns.

Louden, B. (2006). *The Iliad: Structure, Myth, and Meaning*. Baltimore: Johns Hopkins University Press.

Lüderitz, G. (1983). *Corpus jüdischer Zeugnisse aus der Cyrenaika*. Wiesbaden: Ludwig Reichert.

Magen, Y. (2007). "The Dating of the First Phase of the Samaritan Temple on Mount Gerizim in Light of the Archaeological Evidence." In *Judah and the Judeans in the Fourth Century B.C.E.*, edited by O. Lipschits, G. N. Knoppers, and R. Albertz, 157–211. Winona Lake: Eisenbrauns.

Magen, Y. (2008). *Mount Gerizim Excavations. Volume II: A Temple City*. Jerusalem: Staff Officer of Archaeology, Civil Administration of Judea and Samaria; Israel Antiquities Authority.

Magen, Y., H. Misgav, and L. Tsfania. (2004). *Mount Gerizim Excavations, Vol. I: The Aramaic, Hebrew and Samaritan Inscriptions*. Jerusalem: Staff Officer of Archaeology, Civil Administration of Judea and Samaria; Israel Antiquities Authority.

Mason, S. (2007). "Jews, Judaeans, Judaizing, Judaism: Problems of Categorization in Ancient History." *Journal for the Study of Judaism* 38: 457–512.

Mayer, W. (2003). "Sennacherib's Campaign of 701 BCE: The Assyrian View." In *"Like a Bird in a Cage": The Invasion of Sennacherib in 701 BCE*, edited by L. L. Grabbe, 168–200. London: Sheffield Academic.

Meinhold, J. (1909). Die Entstehung des Sabbats. *Zeitschrift für die alttestamentliche Wissenschaft* 29: 81–112.

Mélèze-Modrzejewski, J. (1996). "Jewish Law and Hellenistic Legal Practice in the Light of Greek Papyri from Egypt." In *An Introduction to the History and Sources of Jewish Law*, edited by N. S. Hecht, B. S. Jackson, S. M. Passamaneck, Daniela Piattelli, and Alfredo Rabello, 75–99. Oxford: Clarendon.

Mélèze-Modrzejewski, J. (2001). "The Septuagint as Nomos: How the Torah Became a 'Civic Law' for the Jews of Egypt." In *Critical Studies in Ancient*

Law, Comparative Law and Legal History: Essays in Honour of Alan Watson, edited by J. W. Cairns and O. F. Robinson, 183–199. Oxford: Hart.

Meshorer, Y. (2001). *A Treasury of Jewish Coins: From the Persian Period to Bar Kokhba*. Jerusalem: Yad Ben-Zvi.

Meshorer, Y., and S. Qedar. (1999). *Samarian Coinage*. Jerusalem: Israel Numismatic Society.

Mitsos, M. (1952). "Epigraphai ex Amphiareíou." *Archaiologike Ephemeris* 91: 167–204.

Mor, M. (2011). "The Building of the Samaritan Temple and the Samaritan Governors—Again." In *Samaria, Samarians, Samaritans: Studies on Bible, History and Linguistics*, edited by J. Zsengellér, 89–108. Berlin: De Gruyter.

Noy, D., A. Panayotov, and H. Bloedhorn, eds. (2004). *Inscriptiones Judaicae Orientis*. Vol. 1, *Eastern Europe*. Tübingen: Mohr Siebeck.

Orian, M. (2020). "The *Programma* of Antiochus III and the Sanctity of Jerusalem." *Journal of Ancient Judaism* 11: 200–232.

Peleg-Barkat, O. (2017). "Classical Archaeology in the Holy Land: The Case of Classical Architectural Décor in the Hellenistic Period." In *The Diversity of Classical Archaeology*, edited by A. Lichtenberger and R. Raja, 141–157. Turnhout: Brepols.

Popović, M., M. A. Dhali, L. Schomaker, J. van der Plicht, K. Lund Rasmussen, J. La Nasa, I. Degano, M. P. Colombini, and E. Tigchelaar. (2024). "Dating Ancient Manuscripts Using Radiocarbon and AI-Based Writing Style Analysis." Preprint, arXiv. https://arxiv.org/abs/2407.12013.

Porten, B., and A. Yardeni, eds. and trans. (1986–1999). *Textbook of Aramaic Documents from Ancient Egypt*. 4 Vols. Jerusalem: Hebrew University, Department of the History of the Jewish People.

Rhyder, J. (2024). "Purity, Cult, and Empire: The Proclamation of Antiochus III Concerning the Temple and City of Jerusalem." *Journal of Ancient Judaism* 15: 236–262.

Robinson, G. (1988). *The Origin and Development of the Old Testament Sabbath: A Comprehensive Exegetical Approach*. Frankfurt am Main: Peter Lang.

Rosenbaum, J., and J. D. Seger. (1986). "Three Unpublished Ostraca from Gezer." *Bulletin of the American Schools of Oriental Research* 264: 51–60.

Rosenthal-Heginbottom, R. (2015). "Hellenistic Period Imported Pottery." In *The Ancient Pottery of Israel and its Neighbors from the Iron Age through the Hellenistic Period, Vol. 2*, edited by S. Gitin, 673–708. Jerusalem: Israel Exploration Society.

Runesson, A. (2001). *The Origins of the Synagogue: A Socio-Historical Study*. Stockholm: Almqvist & Wiksell.

Schmid, K. (2021). "How to Identify a Ptolemaic Period Text in the Hebrew Bible." In *Times of Transition: Judea in the Early Hellenistic Period*, edited by S. Honigman, C. Nihan, and O. Lipschits, 281–292. University Park, PA: Eisenbrauns; Tel Aviv: Emery and Claire Yass Publications in Archaeology, the Institute of Archaeology, Tel Aviv University.

Schnabel, E. J. (1985). *Law and Wisdom from Ben Sira to Paul: A Tradition Historical Enquiry into the Relation of Law, Wisdom, and Ethics*. Tübingen: Mohr Siebeck.

Schwartz, D. R. (2003). "Diodorus Siculus 40.3: Hecataeus or Pseudo-Hecataeus?" In *Jews and Gentiles in the Holy Land in the Days of the Second Temple, the Mishnah, and the Talmud*, edited by M. Mor, A. Oppenheimer, J. Pastor, and D. R. Schwartz, 181–197. Jerusalem: Yad Ben-Zvi.

Schwartz, D. R. (2007). "'Judaean' or 'Jew': How Should We Translate Ioudaios in Josephus?" In *Jewish Identity in the Greco-Roman World / Jüdische Identität in der griechisch-römischen Welt*, edited by J. Frey, D. R. Schwartz, and S. Gripentrog, 3–27. Leiden: Brill.

Schwartz, S. (2011). "How Many Judaisms Were There? A Critique of Neusner and Smith on Definition and Mason and Boyarin on Categorization." *Journal of Ancient Judaism* 2: 208–238.

Shalom, N., Y. Gadot, E. Bocher, H. Machline, and Y. Shalev. (2021). "Jerusalem, Givʻati Parking Lot 2017–2018: Preliminary Report." *Excavations and Surveys in Israel* 133. https://hadashot-esi.org.il/Report_Detail_Eng.aspx?id=26089.

Shalom, N., O. Lipschits, N. Shatil, and Y. Gadot. (2021). "Judah in the Early Hellenistic Period: An Archaeological Perspective." In *Times of Transition: Judea in the Early Hellenistic Period*, edited by S. Honigman, C. Nihan, and O. Lipschits, 63–80. University Park, PA: Eisenbrauns; Tel Aviv: Emery and Claire Yass Publications in Archaeology, the Institute of Archaeology, Tel Aviv University.

Sherwin-White, S. (1987). "Seleucid Babylonia: A Case-Study for the Installation and Development of Greek Rule." In *Hellenism in the East: The Interaction of Greek and Non-Greek Civilizations from Syria to Central Asia after Alexander*, edited by A. Kuhrt and S. Sherwin-White, 1–31. London: Duckworth.

Shipley, G. (2000). *The Greek World after Alexander: 323–30 BC*. London: Routledge.

Smithline, H. (2013). "A Unique Hellenistic Pottery Assemblage from 'Akko." *'Atiqot* 76: 71–103.

Stern, M. (1974). *Greek and Latin Authors on Jews and Judaism*. Vol. 1. Jerusalem: Israel Academy of Sciences and Humanities.

Tal, O. (2006). *The Archaeology of Hellenistic Palestine: Between Tradition and Renewal*. Jerusalem: Bialik Institute.

Tcherikover, V. A., ed. (1957–1964). *Corpus Papyrorum Judaicarum*. 3 Vols. Cambridge: Harvard University Press.

Tcherikover, V. A. (1959). *Hellenistic Civilization and the Jews*, translated by S. Applebaum. Philadelphia: Jewish Publication Society of America.

Turner, E. G. (1968). *Greek Papyri: An Introduction*. Princeton: Princeton University Press.

Webster, B. (2002). "Chronological Index of the Texts from the Judaean Desert." In *The Texts from the Judaean Desert: Indices and an Introduction to the Discoveries in the Judaean Desert Series*, edited by E. Tov, 351–446. Discoveries in the Judaean Desert 39. Oxford: Clarendon.

Wellhausen, J. (1885). *Prolegomena to the History of Israel*. Edinburgh: Black.

White, L. M., G. A. Keddie, and M. A. Flexsenhar III. (2018). "The Epistle of Aristeas: Introduction." In *Jewish Fictional Letters from Hellenistic Egypt: The Epistle of Aristeas and Related Literature*, edited by L. M. White and G. A. Keddie, 31–43. Atlanta, GA: Society of Biblical Literature.

Will, E. (1983). "The Recent French Work at Araq el-Emir: The Qasr el-Abd Rediscovered." In *The Excavations at Araq el-Emir, Vol. I*, edited by N. L. Lapp, 149–158. Winona Lake: American Schools of Oriental Research.

Williams, D. S. (1994). "The Date of Ecclesiasticus." *Vetus Testamentum* 44: 563–565.

Wright, B. G., III. (2013). "Torah and Sapiential Pedagogy in the Book of Ben Sira." In *Wisdom and Torah: The Reception of "Torah" in the Wisdom Literature of the Second Temple Period*, edited by B. U. Schipper and D. A. Teeter, 157–186. Leiden: Brill.

Yardeni, A. (2016). *The Jeselsohn Collection of Aramaic Ostraca from Idumea*. Jerusalem: Yad Ben-Zvi.

Yon, J.-B. (2015). "De Marisa à Byblos avec le courrier de Séleucos IV. Quelques données sur Byblos hellénistique." *Topoi: Orient-Occident* Suppl. 13: 89–105.

Zadok, R. (1988). *The Pre-Hellenistic Israelite Anthroponymy and Prosopography*. Leuven: Peeters.

Zadok, R. (2021). "On the Documentary Framework, Terminology, and Onomasticon of the Ostraca from Idumea." In *New Perspectives on Aramaic Epigraphy in Mesopotamia, Qumran, Egypt, and Idumea: Proceedings of the Joint RIAB Minerva Center and the Jeselsohn Epigraphic Center of Jewish*

History Conference, edited by A. M. Maeir, A. Berlejung, E. Eshel, and T. M. Oshima, 179–314. Tübingen: Mohr Siebeck.

Zuckerman, C. (1988). "Hellenistic *Politeumata* and the Jews: A Reconsideration, Review of *The Jews in Hellenistic and Roman Egypt: The Struggle for Equal Rights*, by A. Kasher." *Scripta Classica Israelica* 8–9: 171–185.

Acknowledgments

In researching and writing this book, I greatly benefited from many helpful and enlightening conversations shared with several dear colleagues over the years: the late James Aitken, the late David Amit, Gad Barnea, Andrea Berlin, Wally Cirafesi, John Collins, Yuval Gadot, Shai Gordin, Bruce Griffin, David Hendin, Tal Ilan, Reinhard Kratz, Omri Lernau, Dennis Mizzi, Ronny Reich, Anders Runesson, Zeev Safrai, Peter Stone, Aharon Tavger, Ran Zadok, Karin Zetterholm, and Magnus Zetterholm.

I am grateful to our rector, Professor Albert Pinhasov, and to our dean, Professor Uzi Ben Shalom, for kindly facilitating my research along with my teaching and administrative responsibilities at Ariel University. I would also like to acknowledge the regular support and encouragement of my colleagues at the Department of Land of Israel Studies and Archaeology at Ariel University: Oren Ackermann (our department head), David Ben Shlomo, Adi Eliyahu, Asaf Gayer, Shai Gordin, and Itzhaq Shai. My thanks also go to the manager of our Institute of Archaeology, David Gurevich.

My sincerest appreciation goes out to everyone at Cambridge University Press, who have worked tirelessly to bring this book to print. First and foremost, my thanks go to Aaron Burke and Jeremy Smoak, the dedicated and always accommodating series editors.

And last, but certainly not least, my everlasting love and appreciation go to my family. To my parents, who nurtured a love of learning from an early age. To Netanel, to Emuna and Adiel together with littlest Michal, and to Avital, Techiya, Elyada, and Aviya. And to Sandra and Alexander, to whom this volume is dedicated and without whom it never would have been written.

To Sandra and Alexander, with endless love and gratitude

Cambridge Elements

The Archaeology of Ancient Israel

Aaron A. Burke
University of California, Los Angeles

Aaron A. Burke is Professor of the Archaeology of Ancient Israel and the Levant, and the Kershaw Chair of the Ancient Eastern Mediterranean Studies in the Department of Near Eastern Languages and Cultures at the University of California, Los Angeles, and member of the Cotsen Institute of Archaeology. His research and teaching interests center on the social history of the Levant and Eastern Mediterranean during the Bronze and Iron Ages at the intersections of the study of archaeology, iconography, and texts, including the Hebrew Bible. He has conducted excavations in Jaffa and Tel Dan in Israel.

Jeremy D. Smoak
University of California, Los Angeles

Jeremy D. Smoak is Senior Lecturer in the Department of Near Eastern Languages and Cultures at the University of California, Los Angeles, where he teaches on Hebrew Bible, the history of ancient Israel, and Semitic languages. He is the author of *The Priestly Blessing in Inscription and Scripture: The Early History of Numbers 6:24–26* (Oxford University Press, 2016). He has also published a variety of articles in journals related to archaeology and biblical studies. He has participated in several excavations in Israel and traveled extensively throughout the eastern Mediterranean.

Editorial Advisory Board

Angelika Berlejung, *Leipzig University*
Andrew J. Danielson, *Harvard University*
Marian Feldman, *The John Hopkins University*
Jonathan S. Greer, *Grand Valley State University*
Rachel Hallote, *Purchase College*
Ido Koch, *Tel Aviv University*
Lauren Monroe, *Cornell University*
Stefan Münger, *University of Bern*
Benjamin Porter, *The University of California, Berkeley*
J. David Schloen, *The University of Chicago*
Juan Manuel Tebes, *Pontificia Universidad Católica Argentina*
Naama Yahalom-Mack, *Hebrew University*

About the Series

The archaeology of ancient Israel is among the oldest historical archaeologies in practice. Multi-disciplinary approaches that integrate improved readings of biblical texts, new recovery techniques, pioneering scientific analyses, and advances in identity studies have dramatically changed the questions asked and the findings that follow. Elements in the Archaeology of Ancient Israel embodies these developments, providing readers with the most up-to-date assessments of a wide range of related subjects.

Cambridge Elements⁼

The Archaeology of Ancient Israel

Elements in the Series

Edom in Judah: Trade, Migration, and Kinship in the Late Iron Age Southern Levant
Andrew J. Danielson

Against Moab: Interrogating the Archaeology of Iron Age Jordan
Benjamin W. Porter

Between Yahwism and Judaism: Judean Cult and Culture during the Early Hellenistic Period (332–175 BCE)
Yonatan Adler

A full series listing is available at: www.cambridge.org/EAAI

Printed by Integrated Books International,
United States of America